Education
and
Ethics

Education
and
Ethics

Edited by
WILLIAM T. BLACKSTONE
and
GEORGE L. NEWSOME

UNIVERSITY OF GEORGIA PRESS
ATHENS

Copyright © 1969 by
University of Georgia Press

LC Catalog Card Number: 70-90555

SBN 8203-0234-1

Printed in the United States

Contents

Notes on Contributors

E. Maynard Adams is Professor of Philosophy and former Chairman of the Department of Philosophy at the University of North Carolina. He is the author of essays in the area of ethics and philosophy of mind. His books include *Fundamentals of General Logic* and *Ethical Naturalism and the Modern World View*.

Henry David Aiken is Professor of Philosophy at Brandeis University. He has published widely in philosophical journals. His books include *Reason and Human Conduct, The Age of Ideology*, and *Philosophy and Educational Development*.

Bertram Bandman is Professor of Philosophy of Education at Long Island University. He is the author of *Reason in Education* and articles in both philosophy and education.

William T. Blackstone is Professor of Philosophy and Head of the Department of Philosophy and Religion at the University of Georgia. He is the author of articles on ethics and political philosophy and philosophy of religion. His books include *The Problem of Religious Knowledge, Francis Hutcheson and Contemporary Ethical Theory*, and *The Concept of Equality*.

Robert D. Heslep is Associate Professor of Philosophy and Education at the University of Georgia. He is the author of several articles relating philosophy and education and of *Thomas Jefferson and Education*.

Anthony A. Nemetz is Professor of Philosophy at the University of Georgia. He has authored articles in both philosophy and education and has contributed to *Ethics and Business, Philosophy of Knowledge*, and *Reading the Philosophers*.

George L. Newsome, Jr. is Professor of Philosophy of Education and Chairman of the Department of Philosophy of Education at the University of Georgia. He has authored essays in philosophy and education, and *Philosophical Perspectives*.

Frederick A. Olafson is Professor of Philosophy and Education at Harvard University. He is the author of essays in moral and political philosophy. His books include *Justice and Social Policy; Society, Law, and Morality;* and *Principles and Persons*.

Introduction

EDUCATIONAL institutions, theories, and practices today are under intense scrutiny from a variety of perspectives. Not only are academicians themselves—philosophers, sociologists, political scientists, and psychologists—engaging in this scrutiny, but so also are legislators, businessmen, and the man on the street. There is good reason for this. It is clearly recognized that our educational institutions are to a great extent causally responsible for making our culture and society what it is. They mold and direct the lives of our children; they train persons to fulfill certain roles in society; and they transmit knowledge and values. Given the central role which our educational institutions play in practical affairs, they are necessarily the object of intense interest and controversy.

That interest and concern is even more intense today because American colleges, and universities in particular, are facing grave problems. Campuses across the country and abroad have felt the sting of student protest, and the programs of some universities have been temporarily halted by such protests. The specific causes and objects of these protests are multiple, but behind them lies a general disenchantment with much of our civilization and our educational system. And unlike the hippies who simply "drop out," many student activists want to destroy what they think is an educational system that is unjust, irrelevant to basic human needs, and inadequate. Our colleges and universities stand accused of racism, of collusion with the federal government in international intrigue and various other political and moral improprieties. Some claim that our elementary and secondary public schools have become captives of the middle class which uses the schools to block economic mobility and to intensify class distinctions rather than facilitate the democratization of our society.

There is certainly some basis for these objections. How much is a matter of debate. But it is surely the obligation of the educational institutions who stand so accused to respond objectively to those criticisms and to reassess their activities, aims, and objectives. With this in mind the Department of Philosophy and the College of Education at the University of Georgia decided to sponsor a symposium entitled "Education and Ethics," which would deal with some of the burning questions confronting

education: Is the right to an education a human right? What
constitutes equality of educational opportunity? How can this
be attained in our society? Can we meaningfully confront
the problem of educational equality without confronting the
problem of social and economic equality? What are the moral
rights of youth *qua* youth and *qua* students? To what extent
is it the responsibility of the schools to teach moral beliefs?
Is there an objective test for moral values which can enable
us to decide which moral beliefs to teach? What does it mean
to educate a human being? If education is guided by an image
of man, of what he is and what he ought to be, what is the
proper image? What are the functions of education in society
other than preparing people to perform certain social roles?
Do we not need a program of liberal education which can provide a basis for judgment on the existing social structure,
instead of merely reflecting that structure? Should universities
become instruments of direct political action? What are the
proper limits of student protest? Is the present administrative
structure of some of our universities outmoded and inadequate?

All of these questions are treated in the eight papers which
constitute this symposium held on May 17-18, 1968. The conceptual analysis and normative arguments of the participating
philosophers contribute much toward the solution of these problems and demonstrate the important role that philosophy can play
in educational theory and practice.

W. T. BLACKSTONE
G. L. NEWSOME, JR.

1

Student Activism and the Social Role of the Universities

Frederick A. Olafson

AMERICAN colleges and universities are currently facing a problem of very considerable gravity. During the past five years a movement of student protest has been developing on many campuses across the country; and while most students remain largely uninfluenced by this movement, it can on occasion command wide sympathy within the student population and has succeeded in bringing major universities like Berkeley and Columbia to a complete, if temporary, standstill. The acts of disobedience that have been committed have included violations of both university regulations and statute law; and in the latter case there have often been connections between the on-campus activity of some student organization and the illegal acts which have been committed beyond the campus. Most of the acts in this category have been in the nature of protests against policies of the national government which the participating students believe to be both dangerous and wrong. The question such activities raise for the universities is whether they should penalize students for involvement in such illegal actions that take place outside the university. This question is difficult enough; but the problem raised by acts of disobedience directed against the universities themselves is even thornier. The leadership of the radical student organizations which engage in such actions seeks to compel the universities to alter what is said to be their relationship of complicity with the policies of the wider society which are under attack. To their considerable shock, the universities thus find themselves accused of implicit racism and militarism by reason of their collaboration with the federal government and their financial involvement in the business community; and this challenge comes from within—from a group of students who regard themselves as an exploited proletariat which is entitled to use any weapon in order to compel a corrupt and guilty institution to change its ways. Whatever one may think of these accusations there can be little doubt that they express the sincere convictions of at least a minority of students and the less explicit and intense views of many others; and I think we must also concede that the very strong feelings and beliefs thus engaged are often of a moral character. That fact does not, of course, suffice to justify either these beliefs themselves or the actions to which they lead; but a recognition of the moral inspiration of at least a significant portion of this movement of protest does, I think, create an obligation on the part of universities and those within them who are concerned for their future to formulate their reaction to these events with great care and without undue attention to the side issues and personalities that tend to distort much public discussion of these matters. In this paper I will attempt to make a contribution to this task.

One way to deal with this theme would be to consider the forms of protest currently being used by students as a special case of the more general problem of civil disobedience, and secondly to attempt to develop some judgment on the legitimacy of such disobedience both generally and in this special academic case which has some features that may differentiate it in important ways from other forms of civil disobedience such as that directed against the draft. There is, of course, an initial difficulty here since it is no longer clear that all the disturbances taking place on our campuses are properly classifiable under the heading of civil disobedience. As that term is commonly understood, it designates a deliberate violation of some law or regulation for the purpose of drawing public attention to its iniquitous character through the arrests that become necessary in order to enforce it. Civil disobedience is, of course, distinguished from crime by the public because of the unconcealed way in which it is carried out and by the fact that the persons who engage in it do not seek to avoid apprehension and punishment. It is also distinguished from rebellion by this same avoidance of resistance to the authorities who enforce the statute that is being violated. Whatever persons engaging in acts of civil disobedience may think of the legitimacy of the government in power, their actions do not take the form of an overt challenge to its authority in the way that a rebellion does. Clearly, however, when any element of violence is associated with civil disobedience, the line between it and rebellion becomes much harder to draw; violence in one form or another *has* become a feature of many campus demonstrations. It might well be rewarding to undertake a detailed examination of these distinctions between civil disobedience and crime and rebellion, as well as certain other forms of social protest such as strikes. Nevertheless, while such an analysis might help us to categorize more accurately the disorders that have been occurring on our campuses, it does not seem likely to supply a judgment on the justifiability of these manifestations of student activism or a formula for handling them. There may be, after all, rebellions which are justified and which we should join instead of preventing or suppressing them; and if that is accepted as a premise, then the only way to reach significant conclusions in this matter is to evaluate the case that is being made in their own defense by the student activists themselves.

What I am suggesting, then, is that a judgment as to the way this movement of student activism should be met by the universities requires an antecedent judgment on the goals that movement has set itself. We must ask whether the broad political and social objectives which are being pursued by illegal means are of such importance and are so unlikely to be achieved by other means that would be consistent with a preservation of legality that they must command our support. I am assuming here that breaches of legality *are* involved and that this fact by itself does not suffice to condemn the movement that is responsible for them, although it does create a presumption against it. That presumption could be overturned if a very strong case could be made on general social and political grounds on behalf of the goals of student activism; and if it could, then it would not be enough to judge campus disorders solely in the light of existing rules. Those rules themselves and indeed the university's whole conception of itself would then have to be judged in a higher court of social utility. From that review the revolutionary party might well emerge as the true and legitimate authority within the university and what previously appeared as its illegal actions would have to be reinterpreted as justifiable forms of resistance to a spurious and socially retrograde authority. On the other hand, if it should appear upon careful inquiry that the objectives of the student activists would be purchased at a very heavy social cost without substantial compensating gains, then the universities would be justified in refusing to comply with the demands that are being made upon them. By that I do not mean that the universities would be justified in turning a deaf ear to specific proposals for internal reform or in refusing to create permanent forums in which student views can be presented and discussed. What I do mean is that the administrations would have a right to treat many manifestations of student activism as what in the first instance they are, i.e., infractions of the universities internal regulations; and would have the further right to punish the offenders accordingly.

There is one further respect in which I wish to limit my treatment of the objectives of student activism. I do not propose to discuss those objectives which are in some sense purely internal to the life of the university—matters such as the abolition of parietal regulations, examinations, or admission requirements. These matters are certainly not unimportant and it may be that they enjoy the highest priority among the great mass of the students who participate in campus demonstrations though not, I would guess, among those who lead and organize them. The efforts of the latter, or at least of the most radical among them, are concentrated upon the function of the university within the wider society it serves, i.e., upon the relationship of the university to other institutions in the society and especially to constituted political authority —a relationship which they believe to be a form of tacit collaboration with policies that are both evil and catastrophic. The universities are called upon to change that relationship in a quite radical way and to assume a political and social posture which in the circumstances would unavoidably be one of opposition and challenge to those policies. This is to say that the universities *as institutions,* through the policies they officially adopt and carry out, are to commit themselves to positions which are political in character. By political I do not mean association with specific political party but the identification and sponsorship of concretely defined social undertakings which are needed if we are to realize the goals of peace and democracy of which university presidents invariably speak in glowing terms, but which usually remain quite abstract in terms of what a university may and may not do by way of collaboration with political authority. In short, the universities are no longer to confine their social role to that of an agent of public authority as when they train peace corps workers or carry out medical or military research; and they are not to assume without any real independent judgment that the tasks assigned them by these authorities are in fact in the public interest. I think it is clear, moreover, that the critics whose views I am trying to state are not simply calling for a withdrawal of the universities from their present involvements with government and business, but are advocating the development of new social initiatives which will be consistent with the requirements of a new critical self-consciousness on the part of the university. It is equally clear that when these same critics call for "student power," it is because they believe that the universities will radically change their social role only when effective power within them has been re-allocated in such a way that students acquire a major role in policy formation.

Now some of this has a quite familiar ring to it. Americans, perhaps to an even greater extent than other peoples, have traditionally thought of education as a highly moral under-taking and of the school and the teacher as having a quite special responsibility for the moral development of the citizen and thus of the society as a whole. A conception of the school as the moral crucible of society has found wide acceptance; and some rather extravagant statements on the subject can be found scattered through the literature of American education. Even in the writings of the normally sober John Dewey there occasionally erupt passages of the most unrestrained moral enthusiasm in which Dewey assigns to the teacher and to the school a role that plainly transcends the sphere of normal instructional activity.

The teacher is engaged not simply in the training of individuals, but in the formation of the proper social life . . . . He is a social servant set apart for the maintenance of proper social order and the securing of the right social growth. In this way [he] is always the prophet of the true God and the usherer in of the true kingdom of God.[1]

At the same time, however, it remains obscure just how and through what specific kinds of activity other than inspired class-room teaching this high vocation of the teacher will be realized. There seems to be a kind of gap in Dewey's rhetoric at this point since the more familiar and humbler activities that normally fill a teacher's day scarcely seem to qualify for description in these terms if they are what Dewey has in mind; and if something more is intended, as one is tempted to think it must be, then we are not told what it is. The teacher is consequently left with the grandiloquent assurance that he is a servant of the true God but he still spends most of his time sweeping out the temple. At the same time, it is interesting to note that it is the teacher to

1. John Dewey, "My Pedagogical Creed," reprinted in R. Archambault (ed.), *John Dewey on Education*, New York, 1964, p. 439.

whom Dewey assigns the task of moral and social renovation, not the students. For all this emphasis upon the importance of understanding and utilizing the interests of the student at whatever stage of development he has reached, the role of the teacher remains primary. It is the teacher who embodies the type of free and enlightened intelligence which students are to develop within themselves, and it is the teacher who presides in his own flexible and permissive way over that development. The notion that the authority of even such a friendly and uncoercive supervisor might be found onerous is one that Dewey appears never to have contemplated.

This same primacy of the teacher is even more openly asserted in the well-known essay by George Counts, "Dare the School Build a New Social Order?" which dates from 1932.[2] Counts argues vigorously against the view that the school should maintain an attitude of benevolent neutrality in matters of social concern; and he urges teachers not to try to deny nor avoid the element of imposition, as he calls it, which is necessarily implicit in all education. They should, he says, use the authority that is inherent in their position and in their relationship to their students to build a more humane social order. When read from the perspective of today's events, Counts's plea sounds unmistakably like a demand for "teacher power"; and while he is critical of those who believe that "the school is an all-powerful educational agency, he quite unambiguously calls upon teachers to "reach for power and then make the most of their conquest."[3] He even holds out the hope that "teachers, if they could increase sufficiently their stock of courage, intelligence, and wisdom might become a social force of some magnitude."[4] The schools would then "become centers for the building and not merely for the contemplation of our civilization."[5] This sounds a good deal more radical and more concrete than does Dewey's statement because it really seems as though Counts were proposing that the school become the primary agency for planning and executing the necessary reform of our society. But from this suggestion he draws back. Counts says that his conception of an active social role for the schools does not "mean that we should endeavor to promote particular reforms through the educational system." It turns out that

2. John Dewey Pamphlet No. 11, New York, 1932.
3. *Ibid.*, p. 23.
4. *Ibid.*, p. 28.
5. *Ibid.*, p. 37.

the building of a new social order that is to go on in the schools is really the preparation of those who will issue forth into the world to do the actual building. To this end, "we should . . . give to our children a vision of the possibilities that lie ahead and endeavour to enlist their loyalties and enthusiasm in the realization of this vision. Also our social institutions and practices, all of them, should be critically examined in the light of such a vision."[6] The power that teachers are to seize proves to be power to govern the school and to teach in accordance with their own vision of the social good; and no *direct* intervention of educational institutions in the affairs of government or of other institutions is really being proposed. Again, from the vantage point of our own current preoccupations, it is interesting to note that Counts speaks of a vision that is to be "given" to children and of an enlistment of the latter in a cause that has apparently been defined for them by their elders.

It is clear, I think, that in spite of a rhetorical radicalism which they share with the student activists of today, both Dewey and Counts remain well within traditional conception of the way in which a school or university can properly attempt to influence the policies of the political and other institutions of the society it serves. This is the view that the teacher and the school affect the society as a whole indirectly. They form the mind and character of the child who then issues from the salubrious moral climate of the school and, in the various civic capacities he assumes, proceeds to modify and, if necessary, to reconstruct the society. No doubt the thinking of the teacher or professor and the critical perspectives on society which it proposes will exert an influence on adults as well through the public discussions in which academic figures participate; but, even so, the mediated and indirect character of their influence remains. In short, the university is not itself to be an operational agency in any field except that of education itself; and if Dewey and Counts propose that teachers are to have more power over the school and more freedom to give a political and economic content to the moral and intellectual attitudes they seek to form in children, it is still the latter *in their eventual capacity as citizens* who are to translate their mentors' social vision into social reality.

Now if I have correctly interpreted the statements that have been made about their objectives by leaders of the current movement on the campuses, it is precisely against this limited

6. *Ibid.*, p. 37.

and indirect role of the universities that some of their strongest objections are directed. In part, this impatience may be due to the fact that the "teacher power" movement of the thirties failed, with the result that the universities remain to a considerable extent under the control of the very social authorities whose policies are so repugnant to the radicals of then and now. But the latter are not primarily interested in making the universities self-governing; or rather to the extent that that *is* one of their aims, it is because they expect such an autonomous university to be animated by their own political ideals and controlled to a very considerable extent by them. A university in which student power had become paramount in this way could then be used as an institutional base from which pressure could be exerted upon the unreformed segments of society. In the wilder fantasies of the New Left the university appears to figure as a kind of urban Sierra Maestra from which the student-guerillero will make sorties into unredeemed territory. Once again I hasten to add that this goal which I am imputing to the most radical leaders of student activism is one that very few of their followers and even fewer among those who are influenced by them really share. Most of them have been drawn into that movement by dissatisfaction with one or another aspect of university life which could be corrected within the existing organization of the universities. Still others, perhaps, are expressing through their participation a more diffuse malaise that springs from their bafflement at academic life and their inability to use the university and the opportunities it offers for purposes of their own. But students whose primary complaints are directed against housing regulations or the grading system or even the sheer immensity and impersonality of the modern university rarely mount demonstrations of the kind we have witnessed during the past few years unless these relatively specific discontents have been focused in a general indictment of the universities along the lines I have been describing. There is obviously a certain danger that by turning inward, at least temporarily, to concentrate upon the internal organization of the universities and the current grievances of their immense student populations, the activist movement may lose touch with the wider struggles that are going on outside the universities. A number of observers have in fact pointed out that certain forms of student protest bespeak nothing more clearly than they do a persistence in projecting a child-parent conflict pattern upon all institutional arrangements that involve any element of authority or hierarchy. I do not propose to take up this line of criticism, however, and I will assume that even in this parochial theater of action student activism remains a movement that is directed outward toward the society as a whole. The question I do want to raise is one that concerns rather the effectiveness of the university as an institutional base for radical social reform. In other periods, other institutions have been selected for this role as were, for example, the labor unions in the 1930's; and they have served the purpose assigned to them with very different degrees of effectiveness. As far as I know, no previous attempt has been made in this country or in most others to make the university the *principal* instrument of political action; and the decision to treat it as such undoubtedly reflects the increasing unsuitability and unavailability of the institutions which have traditionally served this purpose. But just how sensible is it to assign this new role to the university and how compatible will it prove to be with older and more familiar functions it discharges?

From the standpoint of their possible function as agencies of social action, our universities as they are presently constituted have one crucially important defect: they are dependent institutions. By dependent I mean that universities derive their resources from the society they serve, and they lack any power, in fact or in law, to command or coerce such support. In the case of publicly maintained universities, this dependency is patent and each year such universities are reminded of it in a rather obvious way when the state legislatures consider their budgets. But even the great private universities with their endowments are heavily dependent for current gifts upon their alumni and upon the government for grants that sustain many research activities. This support, both public and private, is given with the understanding that the universities will operate in a manner that is consistent with legal requirements and that they will not use the resources allocated to them for the purpose of influencing public policy or that of other institutions in any way that has not been explicitly authorized by public authority. There have, of course, been many violations of that understanding, some of which have been tolerated and even encouraged by governmental authorities themselves. It is also hard to draw the line that separates partisan intervention by the university in the affairs of the community from the subtler kind of influence that discussion and research within a university exert over a period of time on public affairs; and the enemies of academic freedom have not been slow to equate the two and to insist that unorthodox thought in a university is tantamount to the treasonable subversion of our institutions. But whatever ambiguities have surrounded this distinction between permissible and impermissible forms of influence by the university within the wider community, its acceptance in some form by the community has been one of the chief safeguards of the freedom that universities effectively enjoy in this country. People, it seems, are not entirely averse to the kind of influence that gradually permeates a society even if it emanates from a university; but they are very quick to resent any institution that officially sponsors and seeks acceptance for policies that involve major social innovation. As a result, American universities have on the whole assumed wider social responsibilities only as the agents of public authority; and they have carefully distinguished between the social views and proposals that are put forward by members of their faculties and the official position of the university as a corporate body which has usually been one of neutrality.

In the eyes of many student activists this neutral posture of the university is its chief sin, and the freedom that is bought at the price of such neutrality is felt to be a degrading form of servitude. To cite just one example of the kind of demand that is now often made on universities and that manifestly requires the abandonment of such neutrality, I would mention a recent denunciation of the university at which I teach for its failure to come out officially against the mayoral candidacy in Boston of a woman whose stand on racial questions was rightly condemned by the critic in question. (In my opinion such an action by the university would have insured her election but that I concede is a tactical consideration and tactical considerations are not currently enjoying a good press among student activists.) In any case, it is very clear that a university could abandon its neutrality and embark upon a program of social activism outside the framework of public policy only if it were prepared to do without a very large part of the support that it now receives. Some private universities might be able to do that although at great sacrifice; but it is scarcely imaginable that a publicly maintained university could survive if it were to adopt such a course of action. There have been a few attempts to found new and, as they are called, "free" universities for this purpose; but as far as I know these have remained largely parasitical upon the established universities from which the members of the free universities seceded. Naturally, I

am not suggesting that survival is always the highest imperative that a university should obey. At the beginning of the
Nazi era the German universities should surely have spoken
out and in their corporate capacity, even if the price had
been their dissolution which would at least have been more
honorable to them than their extraordinary passivity under
a barbaric regime. I would point out, however, that such
action by a university will be largely symbolic in character
though not necessarily ineffective for that reason. A free
university could have survived in Nazi Germany only under-
ground. Happily that is not the situation in our country at the
present time; and the issue that faces us is whether the
university as we know it should be reorganized for another
quite different social role which would entail the sacrifice
of a large part of its current support, and not whether the
university, in order to defend even its present degree of
freedom, must defy the government and challenge the validity
of its laws. Nevertheless, the issue this poses for the universities is quite grave enough; and if a decision to trans-
form the university were to be taken, much thought would
have to be given to the creation of new bases of power and
support for this new kind of university.

A university which is maintained from voluntary outside
sources of support, however inadequately, and which as a
condition of this support is required to remain non-
political in the sense which I have been trying to indicate,
is also a place, at least in intention, in which persons from
quite different groups within the society, with different
political attitudes and different social interests, can come
together for the purpose of study. This is, I concede, the
ideal conception which American universities have of themselves, and a few universities and colleges may in actual
fact have become special preserves in which only those who
are prepared to hew to a given political line are welcome.
But in general this has not been the case; and the student
populations of our universities are probably as diverse
socially as any in the world. Their students unquestionably
segregate themselves in various ways within the universities
and often achieve disappointingly little contact with or
understanding of one another. That fact can hardly be an
argument for abandoning even the ideal of political non-
involvement on the part of the university, however, unless
it can be shown that the impact of life in a university community is in fact negligible from the standpoint of the
political and social issues that dominate our national life.

I do not believe that this is in fact the case, and it certainly cannot be established by such facile arguments as often appear to underly the conviction that the university's institutional neutrality is simply a form of feckless passivity. No doubt the kind of "rationalistic universalism" which our best students often assimilate as a life style in many of our universities often hides a deeper class partisanship which asserts itself when the student assumes his place in the social world, if not before.[7] But there is much to suggest that the attitudes of the educated class, while over-balanced and partially absorbed by the partisan requirements of particular social affiliations, maintain themselves to some degree as a force for moderation, intelligence, and cooperation in our social and political life. If so, and if in spite of the disesteem these virtues are currently suffering we persist in believing that this residue of disinterestedness and universalism is a precious resource in our national life, then we must ask whether they would be likely to receive much encouragement in a sectarian university, so heavily engaged in the social contests of the surrounding society as in effect to invite only one kind of constituency. My own feeling is that they would not and that in this respect what appears from a partisan standpoint as the marginal position of our universities—in the consecrated phrase, their "ivory tower" aspect—is a condition of a distinctive social benefit they confer.

It is not at all easy to imagine what a university that deliberately politicised itself would be like; although it is clear that in matters of support and constituency profound changes would be involved. Nor are there many precedents that can help us to understand what the situation of such a university in relation to society as a whole would be. Nevertheless, the experience of the various Christian churches over the centuries may cast some light on the matter. At the present time, the relationship of most churches to social action and policy is, like that of the universities, indirect in the sense that the church is expected to shape the character and attitudes of its communicants who then, individually and without any authoritative control by their church, are supposed to bring the beneficent influence of their faith to bear on the daily business of life, both private and public. With a few notable exceptions, churches are not themselves agencies engaged in bringing about social and political change; and while churches tend to be classified to some extent as liberal or conservative

7. An interesting discussion of this life-style can be found in *The Academic Revolution* (New York, 1968) by Christopher Jencks and David Riesman, p. 12 *et passim*.

in social matters as do universities, this polarization has not reached yet the point where most churches can expect support exclusively from those who share one or another of these orientations. Not surprisingly, this reluctance on the part of most churches to become directly engaged in political struggles has earned them the contempt of some of their own communicants who have been pressing for a more activistic stance on the part of the churches—a contempt that is justified insofar as the churches' refusal to become involved in social controversy has been a mask for a deeper partisan commitment. I am not concerned, however, to form any judgment on the social role of the churches, but to contrast their present role with others in the past when the church was in some sense an executive social agency. In part by reason of an historical accident—the long hiatus in effective secular government following the dissolution of the Roman Empire—and partly because Christian doctrine claimed a comprehensive control over all aspects of the life of its communicants, the early Christian church assumed direct responsibility, not, to be sure, for social reconstruction in any modern sense, but for a detailed supervision of the lives of its members and in practice of all members of the society. Sometimes this supervision became a direct assumption of the powers of secular government, but later with the revival of secular government the church's position was that of a kind of state within the state, enormously powerful through the financial support it exacted as a matter of right and exerting a steady pressure upon secular government in defense of its own special position which was justified by the church's claim to final authority in spiritual and intellectual matters. Indeed, until far into the modern period ministers of the crown were often drawn from the ranks of the clergy who thus acted in an essentially similar capacity to that of our present-day "in-and-outers," the academics who move so smoothly from the universities into government and back. Of course, the story of the church's involvement in the secular world had an unhappy ending when the revolutionary upheavals of the late eighteenth and nineteenth centuries stripped it of much of its wealth and social power and in many countries returned it to the status of a voluntary private association; and the church was despoiled in this way precisely because it was, and was regarded by the revolutionary party as being, a great and antagonistic social feudality, actively engaged at the primary level of social action in defense of its own interests and its own conception of how society should be ordered.

Now it may seem that the parallelism I am suggesting between universities and churches is fanciful indeed; and so it is in certain obvious respects. The universities in our day are, after all, many, while the church in the medieval period was one. There has been no lapse of secular power that would permit other institutions to intrude upon its normal sphere of competence as there was at the end of the ancient world. And above all the social influence of the church was for the most part profoundly conservative while that of the universities tends to be markedly innovative and liberalizing. But there are equally impressive respects in which these institutions are alike; and among these the most important is a tendency to claim for themselves a kind of monopoly of intellectual and moral authority. This claim, in turn, exposes both to a temptation to pass beyond the confines of a purely advisory role in relation to the executive institutions of society and to assume direct operational responsibilities. In this paper I have been drawing attention to the demands of the student left that the universities move in this direction; but I might equally well have cited the kind of rapprochement of the universities with government that has proceeded so far under the auspices of academics who belong somewhere in the center of the political spectrum—those fabled figures that *Life* magazine has hailed as the "action intellectuals." I am reminded here of Lionel Trilling's charming fantasy in which the walls of separation between government and university disappear entirely and the chief officers of government are known under such titles as "Dean of Defense" and "Dean of State." It would in fact appear that the main difference between left and center activists in this matter of the social role of the universities is that the former envisage the university as an embattled dissenting church and the latter, as an orthodox established church; but both quite emphatically, though in different ways, represent the church militant. The largest question of social policy that seems to me to have been raised by the current unrest is whether the universities *should* be transformed into a kind of secular equivalent of the church militant, whichever sub-variety of the latter appeals to us most.

To that question my answer would be "No"; and my reasons are the very simple and obvious ones that are reflected in the comments I have been making on the activist proposals for the re-organization of the university. As I see it, the universities have two major social duties: the duty to increase human knowledge and understanding and the duty to educate, i.e., to prepare young people to assume positions of special responsibility by helping them to acquire both the specialized competence and the broader critical perspectives which such positions require—ideally, if not as a matter of actual employment criteria. If to these duties we were to add a further require-ment that the universities intervene as independent and partisan agencies in the social and political contests of our time, we would change in unforeseeable ways both the material basis of support for the universities and the social constituencies they serve. It seems very likely to me that these changes would be such as to interfere significantly with the discharge of the first two duties I have mentioned; and that the loss to our society thus entailed would not be balanced by any sub-stantial achievement that can realistically be expected from institutions as weak as our universities really are. They are weak because they have no resources of their own and because they have no natural allies in other social groupings whose strength might compensate for the universities' weakness. In these circumstances, a politicization of the universities could be expected to lead only to their destruction or their suppression and while there are those who accept this consequence and declare that they prefer no universities at all to universities that do not stand in overt opposition to the main trends of our society, their views are not likely to be widely shared. Polariza-tion of opposing points of view may have its utility in the political sphere; but the militance and rigidity it brings with it would be the death of the universities. It seems obvious to me that their demise as free institutions of learning would not benefit the social cause which they would have vainly attempted to serve and that a distinctive institution that contributes in its own way—however indirectly and imperfectly—to the sanity and decency of our society would simply have been sacrificed at the behest of an *enrage* mentality which it is becoming harder and harder to distinguish from the other forms of brutality and violence that fill our lives today.

I wish it were possible to claim that in arguing against these demands I am defending the autonomy of the universities. In a sense of course that is just what I am doing, but I would be less than candid if I left the implication that all would be well and that autonomy intact if only these student radicals would stop trying to push the university into a social role that will make it extremely difficult for it to make its own distinctive sort of contribution. In fact, that autonomy has already been very seriously compromised by the faculties and administrations of our great universities; and I suspect that the demand that the university become engaged in the struggle for radical reconstruction of our society would not have been made or would not in any case have proved as persuasive as it has if it were not for the fact that the universities have so readily accepted a *de facto* alliance with government and industry—an alliance which tends to preserve and strengthen the social status quo at points with respect to which the universities might have been expected to maintain a more independent posture. If student activists were calling the universities back to a saner conception of their own true function instead of insisting that they become engaged on the other side of social conflicts in progress, I would have no criticism to make; and even though they are not, I think it is legitimate to excerpt a negative critique of current university practices from the context of their wider proposals for redeployment of academic resources to another front in the same war. The point of that critique is simply that the universities have not made and apparently have not wished to make effective use of that margin of freedom in relation to other institutions of our society—especially government—which I believe they could validly maintain is theirs. They have been avid petitioners for a share of the public largesse; and they have shown scant concern about the effects of the resulting involvements upon the integrity of their instructional programs and on the possibility of any independent judgment on the public policies in which they cooperate. I submit that it would have been wiser for the universities and in the long run for the country as a whole to assign many of the research and operational responsibilities that the universities have assumed either to governmental agencies or to new non-governmental organizations on the Rand Corporation model which are now being used more and more for this purpose and about which I will have more to say farther on. The object of such a shift would not be to divert them entirely from work in the same areas in which government is and should be active, but rather to insure that the work the universities undertake is dictated by criteria of intellectual interest and long-run social value that are their own rather than those of the clients of such research.

I am aware that the line I am taking makes me vulnerable to the charge that I am separating thought from action; and that is a very serious charge, especially at the present time. It will be said that American universities have long since transcended the limits I seek to impose; and that their vitality and "relevance" are dependent upon their close involvement in enterprises that require an irreversible commitment of thought and resources to the cause of the betterment of human life. This charge has at least a surface plausibility about it since no one can reasonably dissent from the demand that thought and action be effectively related to one another; and it is easy to pass on, as is often done nowadays, to the more questionable claim that intelligence and moral concern can be meaningfully associated with one another only in the context of the kind of undertaking we call a "cause." I would be the last to deny that there have been superb examples of the way intelligence can function within a commitment to such causes; but we all know how often the imperatives of conflict have exerted a distorting influence over thought that is unconditionally subordinate to them. It is, of course, entirely proper that scholars and scientists who concern themselves with matters of public policy should be asked to keep in mind the situation and the priorities of those persons who actually have to make decisions; but this demand can all too easily pass over into a requirement that they keep their inquiries within limits that are dictated by the current strategic convenience of the institution they are to serve. Historically, neither established nor dissenting churches have proved very hospitable to the kind of inquiry that claims the right to ask and to answer questions that may not be convenient from anyone's point of view; and the charge of irresponsibility and lack of social concern has often been used against those who exercise that right. It is being used again today by those who wish to force upon the universities the discipline and the homogeneity that are characteristic of a militant and partisan social force.

There are, over and above these general reasons for rejecting the charge of social irresponsibility, more specific and more specifically contemporary grounds on which a defense of a restricted social role for the universities can be based. As many observers have pointed out in recent years, our society and especially many of our leading national institutions are taking on an increasingly "cognitive" cast. The qualifications necessary for various kinds of work tend more and more to be centered on the certified completion of some course of advanced academic work; and educational level has become a very important element in the assignment of social status. Moreover, business and industry—the traditional hold-outs—have been steadily drawn into this evolution; and research departments and independent research firms of all kinds, drawing on very variegated types of rarefied intellectual expertise, have become a prominent feature of the national scene. To an important extent, technological innovation and economic growth are now dependent upon the contribution that such organizations make. Most of these were the offspring of the universities; and the latter—the original "cognitive" institutions—now find themselves in the company of a growing number of foundations, research firms, laboratories, etc., many of which employ very highly trained products of university study in research activities that are contracted for by private business or government. It seems likely that in the near future many of these organizations and others yet to come will move into the field of social inquiry and planning in a much more ambitious way than they have hitherto done; but here too the organization of work around specific issues of policy will presum-

ably distinguish what these institutions do from the more traditional preoccupations of university scholars.

One large question posed by these developments is what the special position and function of the university is to be within this new
family of "cognitive" institutions and whether the creation of
these new task-oriented research firms does not make possible a
more satisfactory delimitation of the special function of the universities to which, in the absence of these other instrumentalities, a
great many very heterogeneous responsibilities have been assigned.
Many university people view the growth of these non-governmental
firms with considerable reservations, and distrust of the "Rand
mentality" is common among academics. Not surprisingly, con-
tinued activity by the universities in the same fields in which these
firms are working is often regarded as the sole safeguard against
the victory of technocratic intellectuals in the service of big business
and bigger government. But while people in the universities have
an important critical role to play in relation to these new institutions and a yet more important one in training the people who go
on to staff them and while manifold informal relationships between
those institutions and the universities are highly desirable, it is still
clear that universities have a special responsibility which distinguishes them from other "cognitive" institutions and which can be
combined with extensive external responsibilities only with great
difficulty and strain. This is their responsibility to their internal
constituency—their students. I would be inclined to argue that
scholars and scientists who are so interested in pure undisturbed
inquiry or in the actual formulation and implementation of social
policy that they are either ineffective or uninterested in that responsibility should properly find their place in another kind of cognitive
institution, whether a research institute or an operational agency.
The primary social duty of the universities in relation to these task-
oriented agencies and research firms and to government as well is
to prepare the people who will staff them; and while this function is
now often said to place the university in the humiliating position of
a sub-contractor to the dominant industrial and governmental institutions, I cannot see any reason to think that what is apparently
assumed to be the inevitably corrupt character of the latter will
be remedied by an assumption of executive responsibilities by the
universities in the same areas. Nor do I see why, in restricting the
external responsibilities they assume in order to conserve their
resources for their prior social obligations, and in seeking to do
what they can to raise the level of performance in all the principal
institutions of our society by raising the level of training that is
given to those who will staff them, the universities would, in any
reasonable view of the matter, be either cutting themselves off from

the contemporary world or accepting a wholly passive and uncritical attitude toward the performance of the executive agencies they serve.

Returning then to the topic from which I set out, I would offer in the way of a general conclusion the view that the demands that student activists are making for a politicization of the university are ill-advised and that the universities should not yield to such demands. This is not to say that they will be justified or wise in adopting a harsh and repressive policy on the occasion of protests and demonstrations or in turning a deaf ear to what these students —even the most uncivil among them—have to say. And by itself a refusal to yield is not likely to lead to significant changes in the moral atmosphere of our universities unless the latter find ways of re-asserting through important internal reforms their interest in their students and their interest in education. Only by doing so and by associating the training they give with humane and critical perspectives upon the world of practice in which the competencies thus formed will find their place, will the universities be truly justified in saying to the student activists that their distinctive social duty is being discharged and that a policy of promiscuous intervention in the political and social affairs of the larger community would, in addition to its other disabling effects, make the discharge of that duty difficult or impossible.

2

Human Rights, Equality, and Education

WILLIAM T. BLACKSTONE

IN the United States there is very little debate or disagreement over whether the right to an education is a human right or whether all persons should receive equality of educational opportunity. Education is seen not only as a right but as a necessity made compulsory. True, Senator Barry Goldwater and others remind us that the Constitution of the United States says nothing about education; but as Senator Eugene McCarthy points out, it does say a lot about human dignity, happiness, and inalienable rights.[1] Plainly the right to an education or equality of educational opportunity has been taken to be entailed by these fundamental principles. However, there has been and continues to be considerable disagreement over what is *meant* by the human right to an education or equality of educational opportunity, and consequently, over what conditions the fulfillment of which would assure that right or equality.

In this paper I will consider these issues. My procedure will be both analytic, or conceptual, and normative. First, I will present a brief analysis of the general concepts, "human rights" and "equality of treatment." Then I will extend this analysis more specifically to education as a human right and equal educational opportunity. I will also offer several normative arguments and recommendations, which themselves involve reference to recently documented empirical facts, and conclude by giving a brief summary of what I consider to be the limits of the rational adjudication of moral issues of this type.

The analysis offered, I believe, *is* a morally neutral explication. My normative conclusions, though, are the result of two elements: (1) certain value commitments which I think are *essential* for anyone who subscribes to the ethic of democracy, but which go in a certain direction *within* that ethic (what I mean by "within" I will

1. See Eugene McCarthy, "My Hope for the Democrats," *Saturday Review,* November 5, 1966, p. 50.

make clear as I proceed) and (2) the acceptance of certain empirical states of affairs.

I do not think that the concepts, equality and human rights, are identical, though they do cross at important junctures. Historically, equality has been held to be one of several human rights, as by John Locke. Others have held that equality is the only human right. This seems to be what is held by H. L.A. Hart in his thesis that the equal right to be free is the only natural right.[2] My thesis is that equality is used in several different senses, and *one* of those uses is identical to the notion of a *human* right. This is my reason for treating both of these concepts together in this paper. In effect I want to show that the same sort of problems confront the notion of a "human right" as confront the notion of "equality" (that is, a key use of this concept) and, *mutatis mutandis,* the same problems confront the notion of a "human right to education" as confront the notion of "equality of educational opportunity." I turn first to the concept of human rights.

THE CONCEPT OF HUMAN RIGHTS

Presumably what differentiates human rights from legal rights is that the latter are the permissions, entitlements, and prohibitions embodied in statute law and which are enforceable by reference to that law, whereas the former may or may not be so embodied or recognized by law and in fact hold independently of laws or social conventions. Human rights are those rights which one possesses simply by virtue of the fact that one is human. They also hold independently of special acquired characteristics, such as wealth, education, moral character, and so on. No acquired characteristics whatever are relevant, and hence human beings are not gradable in regard to the *possession* of these rights. All that is required is that one be human.

This entails nothing about what constitutes the fulfillment of a given human right for a given person on a given occasion. Human rights theorists have never insisted on identity of treatment as necessary for the fulfillment of a human right. They have insisted that there are multiple grounds which require and justify differential treatment of persons (in fulfilling their human rights), that identical treatment in many cases is improper and unfair, and that consequently careful attention to the circumstances and capacities of persons, and rational *judgment,* is required to properly fulfill a human

2. H. L. A. Hart, "Are There Any Natural Rights?", in *Society, Law and Morality,* ed. Frederick Olafson (Engelwood Cliffs, New Jersey, 1961). First published in the *Philosophical Review,* Vol. LXIV (1955).

right. The fact that one is human therefore, and *qua* this fact possesses human rights, entails little about how one should be treated on a given occasion. It seems to me to entail only that one should be treated as any other human being who is similar to oneself in all *relevant* respects. And this is vacuous indeed until criteria of relevance for differential treatment are spelled out.

The problem, then, as I see it, with the concept of human rights is twofold: (1) criteria for being human must be laid down so that we know which beings have human rights (and though this seems a simple problem I will show in a moment with an example that it is not) and (2) criteria of relevance which justify differential treatment in according a person his human right must be specified.

What are the criteria for being human? Not criteria for being a brilliant, efficient, or productive human but just human? Well, skin pigmentation, the length of nose, and cranium size seem to be accidential features. Are there any essential ones? I am not so sure that human nature has an *essence* which distinguishes it from other animal natures. Perhaps the difference lies in having the capacity or potentiality for a certain range of qualities and activities.[3] Man differs from other animals in that his rational capacities and perceptual apparatus give him this range—the ability to choose, use concepts, and reason—which other animals lack. On this analysis the problem of who is human and therefore has human rights boils down to who has these capacities and potentialities.

What about an imbecile or a moron or a madman? Are they human and do they possess human rights? We say that they do —only that they have impaired capacities. However, and this is the point I want to make here, the notion of "human" can be used in a more flagrantly normative way as Friedrich Nietzsche does when he insists that one is *really* human only if one's capacities are at a certain level—the level of the *Übermensch* or superman.[4] The implication of this for the existence and accordance of human rights is tremendous. In Nietzsche's "master-morality" the scope of rights and duties are severely restricted, depending on one's "slave" or "Übermensch" status. Those persons or bodies without "Übermensch" qualities can in fact be used as a scaffolding for the further elevation and use of those with these *really* human

3. See S. I. Benn and R. S. Peter's discussion of this in *The Principles of Political Thought* (New York, 1964). Originally published in 1959 as *Social Foundations of the Democratic State.*

4. See especially Nietzsche's *The Geneology of Morals* and *Beyond Good and Evil.*

qualities. Everything hangs on what is built into the concept "human."

The Nietzschean thesis can perhaps best be formulated as a choice of criteria of relevance for differential treatment in according rights. That is, instead of simply reading certain bodies out of the human race, the criteria of relevance are set for differential treatment so that the characteristics of "slaves" and "Übermensch" are constitutive aspects of the criteria. Then the rules justify including or excluding or qualifying the treatment of certain persons.

Most anything *can* be justified. It depends entirely on the criteria chosen. The question is which criteria *ought* to be chosen and used, for the question of what is *relevant* is in large part normative. This is the crucially important problem and I will return to it. But first I want to offer a brief analysis of the concept of equality and show that the same problem of justifying criteria of relevance for differential treatment which confronts the notion of human rights also confronts the principle of equality.

EQUALITY OF TREATMENT

I am not here concerned with uses of equality as a descriptive concept but only with prescriptive uses, in particular with the classical principle which has played such a key role in moral and political contexts over the centuries and is formulated by Aristotle in these words, "Equals are to be treated equally; unequals unequally," and by others as "Everyone is to count for one and no more than one" and "all men are equal" (in the sense of being entitled to equal consideration). As with the human rights norm, this principle is vacuous until criteria of relevance for differential treatment are filled in. It prescribes simply that all persons are to be treated alike and that no person is to be given better treatment or special consideration or privilege unless justifying reasons can be given for such differentiation. It prescribes that all human beings, no matter what natural or acquired characteristics they possess, no matter how unequal their endowments and conditions, are entitled to the same relative care and consideration. The principle does not prescribe identical treatment of persons, unless those persons and circumstances are similar in all *relevant* respects. The problem, however, is specifying and *justifying* criteria of relevance for differential treatment. Again, it is plain that everything in the way of the treatment of persons hangs on those criteria. And here is the rub, for these are fundamental differences in the criteria proposed—at least in their order of priority.

Furthermore the claim that certain criteria are relevant involves both descriptive and prescriptive aspects. The descriptive aspect poses no special problem. It amounts roughly to the assertion that certain factors are causally related to given ends, and as such is straightforwardly verifiable. For example, to assert that I.Q. is relevant to educability is to assert such a causal relationship. The prescriptive aspect of judgments of relevance, on the other hand, poses difficult problems. A host of different *general* criteria of relevance has been recommended by Aristotle, Nietzsche, Karl Marx, Franklin Delano Roosevelt, and so on. They include "merit," "need," "worth to society," and so on. Each of these normative criteria can be explicated or unpacked in different ways. Aristotle and Nietzsche do not agree on what constitutes "merit." But let us ignore the ambiguity of these notions for a moment and concentrate simply on the general, contrasting criteria of "merit" and "need." If "merit" is taken as a general and fundamental criterion of relevance for differential treatment, this amounts to the formulation not only of criteria for particular evaluations of how to treat people but also of a general concept of what society should be like. If "need," on the other hand, is given primary emphasis, then we have different guidelines for treating people and a different concept of a desirable society.

I am *not* arguing here that criteria of merit and criteria of need are mutually exclusive. Obviously they are not and one can accept both—and other criteria. It would be an odd world, indeed, in which merit-criteria did not exist. I am arguing that the *moral priority* or emphasis in one's scale of relevant criteria or reasons for differential treatment entails very important differences in guidelines for treating people—for distributing goods and services—and for one's concept of a *desirable* society.

NEED-CRITERIA PRIORITY

Now let us ask this question: Can we justify the claim that need-criteria (admittedly the concept of "need" needs analysis but this is not the place to do it) should take moral priority over criteria of merit and other criteria? For the most part we in this country at least subscribe to this moral priority. We say in a host of contexts, involving medical treatment, legal treatment, basic living conditions and so on that all human beings ought to be accorded a certain mode of treatment *qua* the fact of humanness, *qua* the fact of equality in that sense, and that acquired characteristics, inherited circumstances or rank and wealth, and worth to society are irrelevant in according these modes of treatment. In other words we do, at least on a doctrinal level, espouse the moral priority of need-criteria, and a good case can be made that this priority is fundamental to the democratic ethic. But is there an argument which will justify this priority or must it simply be a fundamental postulate?

There is an argument implicit in Plato's *Republic* which I think is forceful. Plato holds that differential treatment on the basis of merit is inescapable but that fairness requires that, first, all be given the opportunity to develop those meritorious qualities. For Plato this involves the fulfillment of certain basic human needs and educational opportunities. Frankena recently argued the same point, that merit cannot be the most basic criterion for distributive justice because "a recognition of merit as the basis of distribution is justified only if every individual has an equal chance of achieving all the merit he is capable of. . . ."[5] The point is that giving priority to merit-criteria is like pretending that everyone is eligible for the game of goods-distribution, while knowing that many individuals, through no fault of their own, through circumstances and deficiencies over which they have no control, cannot possibly be in the game.

THE HUMAN RIGHT TO EDUCATION

Now assuming that human rights extend to education or that equality extends to educational opportunity, what is entailed by what we have just argued concerning criteria of merit, need, and so on? First, if education is seen as a human right, then all are entitled to it simply *qua* the fact of being human. Criteria of merit, however conceived, such as I.Q. or wealth or social class are irrelevant in regard to the *possession* of this right. Such capacities and conditions are certainly relevant, however, in how education as a right is to be *accorded*. There is no question that these capacities and conditions are causally related to the educability of persons or to the extent to which any given person can be educated. If the above argument on the moral priority of need and capacity-criteria is accepted, then the *ideal* fulfillment of the human right to education entails providing those conditions, social, economic, and educational, which will enable each person to fulfill his capacities. It may be that such ideal fulfillment is impossible in some circumstances—due to extreme scarcity of goods and services. It may be that it is possible but that, for a variety of reasons, available goods and services are not properly distributed. What constitutes proper distribution in

5. William Frankena, "Some Beliefs about Justice" (The Lindley Lecture, University of Kansas, 1966).

any given case is a complex matter of three premises or components: (1) norms or criteria of relevance for differential treatment *and an order of priority* among those criteria, (2) empirical facts which bear on the needs, abilities, and circumstances of the person or persons involved, and (3) knowledge of the goods and service *available* for distribution.

I will not concentrate on knowledge of available goods and services. This is obviously essential for proper judgment about distribution. Since these goods vary greatly from one country to another, this fact alone results in great variability in distribution. It would be unreasonable in practice, for example, to insist on the fulfillment of the right of everyone to a university education in India, whereas it might well be reasonable in the United States. It is conceivable, in fact, that goods of various types be so limited or scarce that the very notion of a right to certain goods or of equality of treatment loses its significance. The same holds for conditions of extreme abundance, for no occasion for pressing a right would ever arise if everyone's needs could be satisfied simply by reaching out or asking. This, I take it, is Hume's point about the conditions which give talk about "justice," and I assume, "rights," its point and significance. Rights talk, then, and claims for equal treatment presuppose conflicts of interests and a world in which there is neither a complete abundance of need-fulfilling resources nor a complete lack of such resources.

Normative Criteria and Empirical Facts

Concerning (1) norms, I have suggested that *genuine* democrats are committed to need-criteria priority, and I will indicate what seems to me to be entailed by this. I want to indicate these entailments by briefly focusing on (2) certain empirical facts or issues.

There are a host of factual issues which must be resolved by sociological and educational research before we can come up with the needed factual premises which, together with our normative principles or commitments, will yield a conclusion about what ought to be done to properly accord the human right to an education or equality of educational opportunity. These facts will vary greatly from one country, or region, to another. My focus here will be on some facts in the United States recently dramatized by the Coleman Report, an 800-page document which is the result of the second largest piece of social science research ever conducted.[6]

6. James S. Coleman, *et al, Equality of Educational Opportunity* (Washington, D. C., United States Government Printing Office, 1966).

A serious obstacle to progress in fulfilling the human right to education in America, and elsewhere, is the absence of adequate, tested information on how well our schools are fulfilling the educational needs of our children and where they are failing to do so. I am not a sociologist or an educational researcher so I cannot presume to tell you what school factors are of central importance in equalizing educational opportunity or fulfilling the human right to education. The variables involved here are exceedingly complex. But the need for reliable information is plain. This is clear from the furor raised by the recent Coleman Report on *Equality of Educational Opportunity*. This survey investigated the relationships of pupil achievement with various aspects of pupil background and some forty-five measures that describe the schools attended. This is undoubtedly the most elaborate data collection project conducted thus far. One of its conclusions, not entirely surprising, is that the differential effects of schools on pupil achievement "appear to arise not principally from factors that the school system controls, but from factors outside the school proper."[7] This report has been criticized for its almost exclusive use of verbal ability as a criterion of academic achievement (a criterion known to be far more a product of a child's home rather than his school). Henry Dyer, Director of The Educational Testing Service, argues that it pays little attention "to the kinds of achievement on which the schools have traditionally focused," and that other criteria in other studies (he cites that of Shaycroft),[8] related specifically to the subjects studied in school, show that among schools there are substantial differences in effects, even when socio-economic differences are accounted for.[9] Dyer concludes that the results of the Coleman Report "have the unfortunate, though perhaps inadvertent, effect of giving school systems the false impression that there is not much they can do to improve the achievement of their pupils."[10]

Now I am not so sure that the Report gives this impression, but the point I want to stress is that we frequently have fundamental disagreements about what can and what cannot be done by schools to insure equal educational opportunity. Much more research needs to be done to provide this essential factual

7. *Ibid.*, p. 312.

8. Marion F. Shaycroft, *The High School Years: Growth in Cognitive Skills* (Pittsburgh, Pennsylvania: American Institutes for Research and School of Education, University of Pittsburgh, 1967).

9. Henry Dyer, "School Factors and Equal Educational Opportunity," *Harvard Educational Review,* Vol. 38 (1968), p. 46.

10. *Ibid.*

data about the key causal factors in the home, community, and school related to educability. In some cases it may be difficult, if not impossible, to separate the variables centering around home and community from those of the school, but we must press our demand for knowledge here to the limit. We desperately need a truer assessment of the key factors related to equality of educational opportunity.

We have known for years that there is massive inequality in public school educaton, which cuts not only along racial lines but also socio-economic lines. Achievement tests show that minority group students of the lower socio-economic class score significantly lower on a variety of tests than middle-class whites, and that far from providing equal educational opportunity, our schools in many cases are not even equipping students to function well in our society. One significant conclusion of the Coleman Report, as I read it, is that we *cannot expect* the schools alone to provide this opportunity, that although the schools can and do mold and shape a student, the *massive* inequality which confronts us can be overcome only by confronting those variables in the non-school environment. As the report points out, the achievement differences between racial and ethnic groups simply are not lessened with more years of schooling.

Normative Recommendations

The upshot of all this is that we cannot meaningfully confront the problem of educational equality without confronting the problem of social and economic equality. Given a social order in which there are very wide differences in living standards, in which even minimal living conditions are not satisfied for a substantial percentage of the population, and in which the children of low income families must become wage-earners in their early teens, the mere formal access to primary and secondary education will never provide equality of educational opportunity. If, *as we profess,* social class and wealth, not to speak of skin pigmentation, are irrelevant in the distribution of education (irrelevant, *not* in the causal sense, but in the sense that they ought not count as factors in regard to the *possession* of rights), then we must institute the necessary social and economic changes which will ameliorate these conditions inherited by so many of our children. More than compensatory programs of education, decreased student-teacher ratios, better facilities, improved teacher quality, and so on are required. Also required are certain fundamental social and economic changes in our society, changes which can overcome the impoverishment and socially hostile-to-education conditions of the home and community.

This is a tall order, and it cannot be done overnight. And we should not make the mistake of seeing the inequality problem as essentially a racial one. There are millions of poor whites and some rich Negroes. What is required is not merely an end to racism but an end to the political powerlessness of poor people, no matter what their color. This will undoubtedly require fundamental changes in the distribution of political power among social and economic classes.

What is at stake is the promise of democracy. Educated and productive citizens constitute the basis of democratic stability, and our public schools have constituted the principal instrument in making such citizens. But whatever success our public school system has had in the past, it is clearly failing today in many instances, especially in many large city ghettos. There is considerable truth in Kenneth Clark's remark that "American public schools have become significant instruments in the blocking of economic mobility and in the intensification of class distinctions rather than fulfilling their historic function of facilitating such mobility. In effect, the public schools have become captives of a middle class who have failed to use them to aid others to move into the middle class."[11]

The cost of changing this in terms of money will be high but we cannot afford not to do it. It will also involve giving preferential treatment to the poor and the deprived; and though this preferential treatment is justified on relevant grounds (given the ethic of democracy), such a policy will result in conflicts of interest, for it will detract from the interest of other classes. It will increase the competition for good jobs and some who now obtain those jobs almost by default may not like the competition.

It will also cost us in terms of freedom. Any new social or economic strictures decrease the area of free choice for man. The 18th century debate on the conflict of equality and freedom did have a point. But again the cost here is worth the product, and we must be willing to admit that on occasion many of our most cherished values do conflict, and choice must be made.

How far are we willing to go in order to remove the causes of inequality? How far should we go? Getting rid of these causes will require a fantastic array of social policies, including birth control, pre-school environment control, housing regulations,

11. Kenneth B. Clark, "Alternative Public School Systems," *Harvard Educational Review,* Vol. 38 (1968), p. 101.

and perhaps a guaranteed minimum income. Our society is clearly moving in the direction of these policies. How far we *will* go can be only a rough guess. How far we *ought* to go requires a continuous debate within the framework of our ethical and normative commitments, one which recognizes that equality of treatment, though a basic value within the ethic of democracy is not the only such value, that there are other basic values such as individual freedom, which may and do conflict with equalitarian considerations and which necessitate a choice, and a loss, *to some extent,* of one of these values. I do not believe that ethical choice is a one-principle affair, and, in my opinion, efforts to reduce all morally relevant considerations to one principle, such as that of utility, have failed. This fact leaves us with the possibility of fundamental conflicts of value, not only with opponents *outside* of the democratic ethic, such as Nietzsche, but *within* the democratic ethic itself. The conflict "within" involves differences not only in priority (or degrees of priority) among criteria of relevance for the differential treatment of persons but also on priority choice when such values as equality *and* freedom conflict.

Metaethical Issues

These comments about conflict of values situations lead me to the final points I want to make. They are conceptual and epistemological points about moral or normative concepts, or what is generally called metaethical issues.

First, neither the notion of a human right nor that of equality of treatment can be reduced to some purely descriptive criterion or set of criteria. To be sure when these concepts are particularized .to some context like education, legal treatment, housing, and so on, various sets of descriptive criteria are formulated which we use as tests for having accorded one his rights or equal treatment. But even in particularized contexts these normative concepts cannot be completely reduced to descriptive criteria. This is at least one thesis that G. E. Moore argued in his talk about a "naturalistic fallacy" in ethics and his "open-question" argument.[12] If Moore's argument has any force, and I believe it does (though we need not be led to talk about "non-natural" properties by it), it applies to the concept of "equal educational opportunity" just as much as to the concept of "good." Suppose, for example, educational equality is explicated or defined in terms of (a) the racial composition of the school or (b) the community's input to the school, such items as per-pupil expenditure, school

---

12   G. E. Moore, *Principia Ethica* (New York: Cambridge University Press, 1903).

plants, library, and so on, or (c) the similarity of the educational results of the school for individuals with similar backgrounds and abilities, or (d) exposure to a common curriculum, and so on. These are some of the senses of equality of educational opportunity discussed by Coleman. The point of the "open-question" argument in the educational context and of the naturalistic fallacy accusation is that it makes perfectly good sense to ask whether a person has been accorded equal educational opportunity or his right to an eduation even if (a) or (b) or (c) or (d) is the case. These criteria may all be valid ones for assessing equality of educational opportunity but no one of them or all of them *constitutes* the meaning of educational equality. Of course, there may be *some uses* of the notion of equality of educational opportunity which are explicable entirely in terms of descriptive criteria—in the same way in which *some uses* of "good" can be explicated descriptively. But in most uses there is a commendatory function or a normative dimension which cannot be so reduced. It is part of what might be called the logic of the concept that it cannot be so reduced, that it cannot be defined for all time in terms of necessary and sufficient conditions. Both the normative ideals in the concept and the material conditions necessary for implementing the ideal change with time and place. There is no escaping the necessity for judgment both in regard to the content of the concept itself and of the application of it in a concrete situation.

Finally, with reference to my comments on value conflicts "inside" and "outside" of the democratic ethic, I want to indicate, all too briefly, and hence dogmatically, the limits which I believe exist in the justification of human rights and equality claims. These limits, I think, apply to moral conflicts in general, and my comments here constitute part of a metaethic not fully developed in this paper. My concern here is with the normative premises in these claims.

First, it is plain that even if a case can be made out that the very concept of equality or human rights as explicated in this paper is *constitutive* of adopting a moral point of view at all (as opposed to prudential, etc.); that is, even if it could be shown that moral discourse is logically impossible without presupposing the equality principle, this does not take us very far. Some philosophers do just this,[13] and I feel sure that non-equalitarians will quickly shout that this is a case of surreptitiously smuggling in a norm under the guise of a neutral philosophical analysis of the notion of a moral point of view. This issue I

13. See R. S. Peters, *Ethics and Education* (Glenview: Scott, Foresman and Company, 1967) as an example, especially p. 49.

will not discuss now. Even if the claim is true that equality is
constitutive of moral reasoning, all the substantive problems
centering around different criteria of relevance for differential
treatment remain.

Secondly, I am convinced that a descriptivist account of
human rights and equality claims is false. Equality and human
rights are not descriptive properties of humans. Nor are they
somehow embedded in the marrow of reality, from which we can
somehow read them off. Nor are they directly inferable from
properties possessed by humans, such as "reason." For if reason
is a descriptive property, we cannot logically infer any rights or
norms from it alone. If reason, on the other hand, is a normative
concept with the notion of rights built in, so to speak, then no
inference is necessary. The problem is either the "is-ought"
gap or circularity.

If I am correct that a descriptivist metaethic is mistaken
(which I have not here supported by an argument), that human
rights and equality are not norms which are somehow *discovered,*
then a number of natural law theorists and others who feel the need
for metaphysical underpinning for moral norms may be dis-
appointed. Having some of these inclinations myself, I feel
at least a twinge or tug. However, these norms and the segment
of moral discourse which accompanies them can be given a *kind*
of justification in another direction; so we need not be committed
to some sort of complete scepticism concerning them. That
direction is simply a pragmatic justification. One can point
out that these norms are absolutely essential as instruments in
effecting a certain type of society, that they can be given up
only at the very high cost of precluding that type of society.
This is parallel to H. L. A. Hart's argument that the language
of special and general rights logically presupposes the equal
right of all men to be free, that consequently one can give up
this latter principle only at the cost of giving up an entire
segment of moral discourse and its concomitant practices.[14]

Some persons, finding undesirable the kind of society made
possible by the wholesale endorsement of human rights and
equality, would be unconvinced by this type of argument. That
is the weakness of any pragmatic argument, but it may well be
all that we have.[15]

14. H. L. A. Hart, *op. cit.*
15. I emphasize the word "may" here. I do not want to rule out the possibility of other
arguments justifying the equality principle. In fact, in a forthcoming article ("Human
Rights and Human Dignity," *The Philosophy Forum,* Vol. 9, 1970) I set forth such
arguments, in effect offering a half-way house between natural law theory and pure con-
ventionalism.

3

Ethics and the Aims
of Education

E. Maynard Adams

EDUCATION, by the very meaning of the word, is concerned with drawing out, eliciting, evolving, and developing latent powers. But insofar as it is intelligently pursued and promoted, education must be guided by some image of the evolved or developed product. The image may be restricted or distorted, thereby narrowing or perverting the educational process. It is my claim that education in America today suffers from both of these defects.

Vocational and professional education is guided by a limited image. We have very definite and specific concepts of what it is to be a carpenter, an architect, an accountant, a mathematician, a lawyer, and the like. We can devise effective programs of training and education to develop the required competences, for we know more or less what we are after and when it has been achieved. We can experiment with programs and methods and eliminate the ineffective and steadily improve the successful. But even vocational and professional education cannot be content with merely success in terms of their limited goals. Any school, however specialized, in recommending its graduates must evaluate them not only with regard to their specialized competences but as human beings. No one wants a mechanic, lawyer, or physician, however competent he may be in his specialty, if he practices his trade or profession in such a manner that he is open to condemnation as a person.

Our concern here is with the education of human beings rather than carpenters, lawyers, chemists, and the like. Liberal education, guided by the image of man, is given to this task. It is more fashionable now, and has been for some time, to talk about general education. I suspect the shift came about in search of a guiding image. Having no clear conception of an educated man, we attempted to define a goal by taking the common denominator of the various vocational and professional educational programs. Thus general education attempts to develop the common skills and knowledge required by all the specialties. If a high school student does not plan to go to college to prepare for a learned profession or vocation, it is often thought that he should not waste his time on the so-called general education subjects but go immediately into some practical vocational program. Our educational program is largely oriented, either directly or indirectly, toward vocational and professional education.

Our society supports education primarily to prepare people to perform certain functions in society just as it builds machines to do certain jobs. Education is part of the society's capital investment. The social system, with its needs, determines for the most part the goals of education. Men are shaped to fit into and to serve the needs of the system, which tends to have a life of its own superior to that of the people.

Insofar as the system is justified in terms of external values, appeal is made to its capacity to provide people with material goods and services. People are encouraged to seek an education in order to prepare people for the jobs in the system. Much of the pressure from within for reform of the system is to provide more and better jobs in order to give the people more purchasing power with less effort and under more pleasant conditions. For the most part, we place a higher value on our material standard of living, possession and use of the products of technology, than anything else. Anything in the way of technological progress must go; everything required for technological progress is embraced. And the sole justification for technological progress is that it advances our material standard of living. The dominant vision our popular culture gives our youth is that of a glamorized life of pleasure and a higher position in the economic order so that they can enjoy more of the products of technology. We are deeply disturbed by the segment of our population in the so-called poverty cycle. They have no motivation to escape it by the approved methods of the society. We have a crusade on to convert them. They are the lost ones, for they are not destined to our culture's heaven. The same zeal that used to go into saving souls from hell is now given to saving people from poverty. This is what is meant when it is said that ours is a materialistic culture.

There is a widespread uneasiness and concern in our society today that all is not well. Editorial writers say that everywhere we look something is wrong. But most popular diagnosticians look at only superficial symptoms like our international difficulties and the poverty and violence in our cities. Our problems cut much deeper. Even if we could achieve a genuine peace in the international community and solve the race and poverty problems at home, we would still have all the problems inherent in our democratic, middle-class technological civilization. There is perhaps more profound lack of morale today among those fully participating in the best that our society has to offer than in the Negro ghettos of our decaying cities.

We can understand the despair and frustration of those un-equipped to pull their weight in our complicated, industrial society and separated and crowded out of sight in unbelievable squalor. We know in general how their peculiar problems can be solved. They must, we think, be brought into the mainstream of American life so that they can participate fully with others in the riches of our civilization.

But the increasing restlessness, frustration, despair, and rebellion of those who have made it in our way of life, those who are prepared to and have participated fully in the best that our civilization has to offer, are much more difficult to understand and far more alarm-ing. We have been through a generation of despair and sickness of spirit. This is reflected for all to see in the great mirror of the spirit of our culture—our art, literature, and philosophy. And there is the disenchantment and rebellion of our younger generation, espe-cially the best educated from the upper middle-class families. The beatnicks and hippies are the most extreme. They repudiate our civilization and have dropped out of our society. The new radical activists are not content to drop out. They want to tear our society down, including our educational system, for they believe it to be rotten to the core. They believe that people are sacrificed to the efficiency and goals of an over-developed technological and bu-reaucratic system. Although these extremists may not be large in number, they seem to be expressing a widespread spirit of discon-tent and a rebellious attitude that is just beneath the surface. It is widely felt that our culture, including our educational system, is perverting man and is irrelevant to basic human needs.

An educational system consisting for the most part of voca-tional and professional education and their supporting general education largely serves the ends set by the existing society and does little toward basic criticism and reconstruction of the society itself. The vocations and professions in the society, the jobs to be per-formed in the existing social structure, determine the goals of education. They provide the dominant guiding images of the educa-tional process.

What is needed is a program of liberal education fundamentally independent of, although not irrelevant to, the vocational and pro-fessional needs of the existing society so that it can provide a basis for judgment on the existing social structure and the vocations and professions it makes possible. The only way this independence can be gained is for the educational program to be guided by an image of an educated man that is independent of particular vocations and professions, indeed independent of even the common requirements for the various vocations and professions. However, a liberal education program based on a false or perverted image of man might work more havoc than general education geared to vocational and professional needs. It is my conviction that this is probably true of what we now have in the way of liberal education, and we have some that is distinct from general education. Indeed, a vigorous effort is underway, guided by what I regard to be a perverted image of man, not merely to reform but to revolutionize our educational programs and our culture. What I mean will be made clear a little later.

To speak of an educated man, in the sense our line of thought suggests, requires that the concept of man function much like the concept of a vocation or of a profession. We know something of what it is to be a well-educated physician or lawyer. It is simply to have acquired through instruction, training, study, and practice the knowledge and skills that enable one to function well as a physician or lawyer. But can we even talk meaningfully about a well-educated man? About one who has acquired the knowledge and skills that enable him to function well as a man? The answer to this question must be found in how we talk about man, in what it makes sense to say about him, especially in the way of appraisals.

Let us look at moral appraisals. They are distinguishable, I suggest, from certain other kinds of evaluations of what one does because they reflect upon the agent as a person rather than as a carpenter, a physician, or the like. Some judgments of wrong-doing may be used to back a claim that the person concerned is a poor surgeon, others that he is a bad business man, etc. But some things that one does wrong may be used to back the claim that he is "no man at all," "a poor excuse for a man," "a despicable man," "an immoral man," "an unjust man," "a wicked man," "a depraved man." Likewise, some things that one does right may be used to back a claim that he is a good surgeon, a good accountant, or the like; others may be used to back the claim that he is a "good man," "a just man," "a virtuous man."

I am not urging that we define a moral appraisal of an action as one that reflects on the agent as a person. Indeed, there are nonmoral appraisals that so reflect on the agent, e. g., charges that an act is a stupid thing to do, illogical, etc. All I am saying at the moment is that moral appraisals of action necessarily reflect on the agent as a person and thus reveal something about the nature of man or our implicit image of him.

It has often been remarked that moral judgments are universalizable in the sense that whatever is right for one person to do would be right for any other person under similar circumstances. There is something logically wrong in morally condemning in the conduct of another just what one approves in one's own behavior or vice versa. The reason for this is that the moral appraisal of an action bears upon it as the act of a person in such a way that the identity of the person is irrelevant except insofar as some identification of the agent may be essential for a full description of the action being judged.

Talk about rights is especially revealing. On first thought, it might seem that a person's rights are of two kinds, namely, those grounded in a responsibility of another and those grounded in some legitimate purpose, function, or responsibility of one's own. The right of a wife to support from her husband or of a son to share equally with his brothers and sisters in his father's estate might seem to be examples of the first kind. The rights of one by virtue of an office he holds, e.g., the presidency of the United States, are clearly of the second kind. The controlling factor is the function of the office, the responsibilities of the officeholder, the imperatives that define the position. The rights pertaining to the office are the areas of freedom one must have in order to be able to fulfill the legitimate purposes, functions, and responsibilities of the office. Of course, the areas of freedom required for others by their respective legitimate purposes, functions, and responsibilities impose a limit on the rights of the officeholder and thus are indirectly controlling factors.

It seems clear that the apparent distinction between the two kinds of rights does not hold up under examination. No one has a responsibility to another except insofar as the other has a valid claim on him. It is the claim that is basic. It generates or constitutes the correlative responsibility. The wife has a right to support that imposes the responsibility on the husband. The responsibilities of a parent are imposed upon him by the rights of the child. One's human rights are not grounded in the responsibilities of others or of society in general, but rather in one's own purposes, functions, and responsibilities as a human being.

Thus, talk about human rights suggests that to be a human being is somewhat like having an office, namely, to have some purpose, function, or responsibility and the correlative rights and privileges.

We may conclude that moral talk about man and his behavior reveals a concept of man that defines for him a way of life much like the concept of a physician defines for one who is a physician a job to do. One who has no sense of identity, one who has no concept of who he is, is incapable of moral judgment. One who makes moral judgments with confidence has a clear sense of identity. He has a concept, however implicit, of what it is to be a human being who is logically involved with his moral appraisals. Some would say that it is the concept of man that makes moral appraisals possible. In a sense this is true. But it is also the case that our specific concept of man is under the control of our moral appraisals of human conduct.

The concept of a human being that is relevant here is not one that could be expressed in a formula such as "anything is a man if and only if it is F, G, and H." A concept of this type is not true of something that fails to have the specified properties. The concept of man is like a functional concept, e.g., "knife," "pump," "carpenter," "physician," etc. It is normative in character. It has some such form as this: anything is O if and only if it is F and G and ought to be H. O could be true of something that was not H. It would, however, be a defective O. A knife ought to have a cutting part, usually a blade, but something without one could still be a knife even though a broken one.

Hare, in *Freedom and Reason* (R. M. Hare, *Freedom and Reason*, Oxford University Press, 1963), contends that moral reasoning is of two types, utilitarian and idealistic. Utilitarian reasoning, he says, is under the control of inclinations in a way somewhat parallel with the way Karl Popper contends that scientific hypotheses are under the control of sensory experiences. One may find that his moral judgment, when its logical consequences are fully developed, is in conflict with some inclination he has or would have under certain imagined conditions and thus is unacceptable to him. But an idealist, Hare says, reasons from his ideals of human excellence. He judges actions as fitting or not relative to his image of the ideal man. Such judgments, he contends, are not subject to refutation by any dimension of experience. For this reason, he labels the idealist a fanatic.

In the first place, moral judgments are not unacceptable because of conflict with inclinations. If they were, they would be of little value to us. Their most distinctive function is to override inclinations. We may disapprove of or judge it wrong for one to act on a certain inclination in a given situation. This is not simply a judgment to the effect that the consequences would be contrary to some set of wants or inclinations, but rather a judgment that the act, in light of its known consequences, would be an inappropriate thing for the agent or any man to do under the circumstances. It might be something we would not condemn in a child or a tiger even though the consequences were the same. Even according to Bentham, the fact that utility is the principle of moral judgment means that man, by the natural constitution of the human frame, operates under the utilitarian imperative. In other words, the ideal for man is the utilitarian life. An act contrary to the principle of utility is unbefitting a man. Thus even the classical utilitarian is an idealist in Hare's sense.

Does this mean that the utilitarian is also a fanatic? Are they free

from all experiential controls? Surely ideals of human excellence
are grounded in such experiences as admiration, feelings of guilt,
esteem for oneself and others, approval and disapproval, and the
like. No doubt ideals, once formed, color and shape such experiences, but nonetheless they are tied to and shaped by such experiences. They arise out of them and are constantly changed by them.

But what is the status of the concept of man revealed by an analysis of moral appraisals? A natural law moral philosopher like
Plato or Aristotle, or even a utilitarian like Bentham, would say
that there is one and only one correct concept of the objective
essence or natural constitution of man. A subjectivist like R. M.
Hare or Jean-Paul Sartre would say that man has no objective
essence or natural constitution to be discovered. He has no identity
as a person until he defines or constitutes himself by an unreasoned
commitment to a principle that defines for him a way of life. In
such a commitment, Sartre would say, one defines not only his individual self-hood but invents man; that is, he lays down the basic
principle that makes possible moral appraisal of himself and others.

The issue here is whether moral appraisals proceed on the basis
of discoveries made by the exercise of our natural faculties or
whether they are made possible by and are relative to a decision
of principle, as Hare would say, that is unguided by moral experience and reasoning, and, indeed, makes moral experience and reasoning possible.

If the latter is true, the concept of man revealed at one level of
analysis of moral appraisals will vary from culture to culture and
indeed from individual to individual, for each man, according to
the theory, makes his moral appraisals in terms of some basic imperative he accepts, whether by cultural influence or by his own
volition, that defines for him the concept of man. At a deeper level
of analysis the concept revealed is that of a completely free mind,
a bubbling well of consciousness, that must invent man, that must
without guidelines define a way of life by a decision of principle.

An educational program even partly shaped by a concept of man
revealed by the first level of analysis would be, according to this
view of morality, repressive and enslaving. It would impose upon
everyone so educated a way of life defined and constituted by the
volitions of others and thereby rob them of their freedom and individuality. An educational program shaped by the concept of man
revealed at the deeper level of analysis, according to this view,
would work toward freeing the individual from any cultural image
of man that defines for him a way of life. It would teach that the
structure of society—its customs, institutions, and laws—is simply
a residue of the sentiments and volitions of others and therefore a
threat to an individual's freedom and individuality, that the indi-

vidual in society must not acknowledge any authority nor feel obligated to obey laws and policies of the society, that he must rebel, free himself, and follow only his own will. On this view of man, all authority collapses into naked power and all law into oppression.

Although belief in the subjectivity and personal character of moral judgments gives rise to the death of all authority and to resistance to the established ways of society on the part of individuals in search of their personal identity and authentic existence, it naturally leads to efforts on the part of society to control the attitudes and moral judgments of people, for these are their springs of action. Where there is no conviction that free inquiring minds will move toward agreement by discovering an objective truth, it is felt that propaganda, indoctrination, censorship, speaker bans, and the like must be employed to safeguard and to protect cherished institutions and ways of living, indeed to assure that minimum consensus in attitudes and judgments necessary for society to function at all.

I think it is undoubtedly true that what liberal education we have in America today is largely built upon these assumptions about man. The present discontent and revolutionary spirit among our youth is not only a product of a vague uneasiness about the human relevance of our vocational and professional oriented education with its supporting general education, but also a product of a heightened sense of oppression created by a change in our conception of man and morality, a change most pronounced among sophisticated circles in our educational institutions but rapidly pervading our whole culture. It is not just that the existing structure of our society is felt to be oppressive. Any established order with its cultural values would be regarded as oppressive. According to Sartre, the free man is one who recognizes no authority and feels no restraints or obligations from any source other than his own will, which he regards as subject to nothing, not even an objective situation. There are no requirements or guidelines. Everything is permitted. To grow up, to become a free man, is to be able to do what one wants to do without any felt inhibitions or restraints.

In light of our cultural climate, there is little wonder that homes and schools are battlegrounds between the generations, that there is a youth revolution stirring in the land, that all establishments are under attack. We have a materialistic civilization and supporting educational program that seems to be fragmenting and perverting man to such an extent that many are dropping out or resisting. Furthermore, our liberal education is largely based upon a conception of man that accentuates our discontent with our present culture but provides us with no basis for correction and reconstruction of our social and cultural order. It provides a basis only for revolution and anarchy, which means of course that tyranny would follow.

It seems clear to me that the conception of man revealed by the Hare-Sartre theory of moral appraisals not only leads to undesirable consequences, but that it is false. Beginning with the assumption that moral appraisals cannot proceed on the basis of discoveries made by the exercise of our epistemic powers, the theory attempts to make sense out of moral discourse. And, given its basic premise, it does about as well as is possible. But the assumption on which the theory is based may be questioned. Value language is almost universally recognized to be the language of emotion, passion, enjoyment, suffering, and volition. In some way it is tied in with this dimension of experience. Whether moral judgments, indeed the whole range of value talk, have an objective ground turns upon the character of this mode of experience. Is it epistemic in its own right? Do we through our enjoyment and suffering, desire and aversion, and various emotions and passions and their appropriate modes of thought discern and know a dimension of reality not accessible to us through sensory observation and scientific thought? Here lies the heart of the matter.

The only way to determine whether value experience is epistemic is through an examination of what it is meaningful to say about it, for this reveals its categorical structure. If our epistemic team of concepts, which includes semantic, logical, seeming, and justificatory concepts as well as straightforward, full-blown epistemic terms, meaningfully apply in a literal way, just as they do to sensory observation and the thought grounded in it, then we must admit that it too is knowledge-yielding and that reality is not restricted to what is knowable through sensory observation. It is my conviction that this is precisely the case.

Let me briefly sketch three of the major considerations which support this claim.

(1) Our feelings, emotions, attitudes, and even desires are linguistically expressible in much the same way as our perceptual experiences, dreams, and thoughts in general; that is, we can put into language the semantic content of all these modes of experience and thought. We can say in language what is experienced or thought. This is not, I suggest, unlike expressing in French what is before us in English. It is a form of translation.

We express our feelings, emotions, and attitudes in straightforward value judgments. One may express his enjoyment of a dinner by saying that it was good, his guilt feelings by saying that what he had done was wrong, his sense of obligation by saying that he ought to do *X,* his disapproval of someone's action by saying that he ought not to have done it, his anxiety by saying that such and such may not turn out well, his hope for X by saying that X is possible and that it would be good if it were to happen, and the like. This is not unlike expressing what one sees by saying such things as "He is now turning left onto Rosemary Street," "A car is entering our driveway," "The two men are standing face-to-face and seem to be engaged in a heated argument," and so forth.

Even our desires lend themselves to linguistic expression or translation. One may express a desire for X by saying that it would be good if it were the case, or in the imperative form, "Lubricate the car and check the brakes," "Let's stop at the Hilton," and the like.

The fact about our affective and conative experiences which I am trying to point up, namely, that they embody a semantic, a meaning, a dimension is indicated also by the language we use to report such experiences. We report a particular speech act, for example, by saying "Mr. X said that his company's profits were up fifteen per-cent this year." Note that the verb 'said' is transitive and that its object, the subordinate clause, is in propositional form. Its meaning, its content, is what the speaker puts into words in expressing himself. We may use the same linguistic form to report a feeling or attitude with the subordinate clause formulated in value language. For example, "He felt that X would be wrong." We may, of course, report feelings and attitudes by such locutions as "He was disgusted with the whole affair," "He was overjoyed by the news," and the like. These reports, I think, can be translated respectively without much distortion into "He felt that the whole thing was a shabby, inexcusable affair" and "He felt that the news was extremely good."

If value experiences have the semantic dimension indicated by these linguistic considerations, then analysis of value language must locate what it means within the semantic content of such experiences, just as we locate what is meant by color language in the semantic content of visual experience. But this is not enough. We want to know not only whether value language has a semantic meaning that is locatable in experience, but whether the semantic content of both value language and experience has an independent status, whether it is locatable in reality, in the objective world. I suggest that this question is to be settled by assessing value experience epistemologically to determine whether it is knowledge-yielding. The fact that there are value experiences with a semantic dimension in judgmental form is a necessary condition but not a sufficient one.

(2) Another consideration, which is essential in determining the epistemic character of value experiences, is whether they

are subject to logical appraisal in a way similar to sensory perceptions and thought in general. This I find to be the case. There are disagreements in our feelings, attitudes, desires, purposes and the like as well as in our sensory experiences and beliefs. No one can look at the world at large or at his own personal life without having this fact impressed upon him. Part of this disagreement in our value experiences may be grounded in objective, conflicting requirements inherent in the human situation. But much of it is in experience only. Such disagreement is logical in character; it is a form of inconsistency. If a person wants very much to do something and yet regrets having done it after the fact, there is a logical incompatibility between the want and the regret. We give a privileged position to the regret and thus one would conclude that he had been mistaken in wanting to do it. If we suddenly become excited about some possible course of action and want very much to undertake it, we think that it is the course of wisdom to sleep on it to see if our feelings about the matter over some period of time and in light of a full consideration of all the facts will be consistently for going ahead with it. Quite often we find that our later feelings about the issue are actually incompatible with our initial enthusiasm. If so, the later sentiments are regarded as correcting the earlier ones. We are in fact disturbed, in spite of our professions of open-mindedness and tolerance, when the feelings and attitudes of others whom we respect are incompatible with our own. If the disagreement is unresolved, it either undermines our own feelings and alters them or else we tend to discredit the other person in some way and thus to alter our respect for him. In a word, we tend to safeguard our own feelings and sentiments by casting suspicions on the reliability of the feelings and value judgments of those who disagree with us. Furthermore, it is very easy to do this by questioning the character of those who oppose us, for, as Aristotle said, only the good man can know what is good and right. Thus those whose value experiences and judgments disagree radically with our own are likely to be regarded as wicked enemies. All of this, I think, supports the claim that there are logical relationships among our value experiences and that such experiences are subject to logical appraisal in much the same way as perceptual experiences and ordinary thought.

(3) What has already been said about the semantic and logical character of value experiences supports the further claim that a value experience may be meaningfully spoken of as refuted or corroborated, as in error or as correct. Furthermore,

it makes sense to say that one has good reasons for feeling the way one does about something, that his sentiments are rational; or it may be said that one's feelings are unfounded, that they are invalid or irrational.

Because it is meaningful to talk about value experiences as expressible in language in the way we do, as logically consistent or not, as being corroborated or refuted, as being correct or in error, as grounded in reason or not, as rational or irrational, and the like—because it is meaningful to talk about value experiences in terms of this team of epistemic concepts, I conclude that this dimension of experience is knowledge-yielding in much the same way as our sensory experience and thought grounded therein.

This opens up for us a whole new dimension of reality, namely, objective values. Let me say just a word about what they are. The only way we can get at the structure of a fact is through the form of a philosophically clarified statement that asserts it. In like manner, we can get at what a value is through the form of value judgments. I suggest that "ought" judgments are basic. Predicative value judgments like "X is good," when philosophically clarified, become something like "X is more or less the way it ought to be." "Ought" judgments themselves need clarification. To say that X ought to be F is to say that there are reasons for X to be F, or, what amounts to the same thing, that there are facts in the situation which normatively require X to be F. The most satisfactory linguistic form for a value judgment, then, is something like this: "If X is X, then X (or Y) ought to be G;" or "If X is F, then there ought to be a Y that would be G." The normative tie, requiredness, I suggest is locatable in the semantic content of our feelings, emotions, and desires. If we fail to look here, which most have done because this dimension of experience is widely taken to be nothing but causal reactions to the reality discerned through sensory observation, then we cannot find in either experience or the world what seems to be meant by value language. But I urge that it can be found here and if value experience is epistemic as I have contended, then normative requiredness is an objective reality.

Perhaps the major consideration against this position is the uncertainty and variability of our emotive and conative experiences. Many have felt that such experiences speak, if at all, in too conflicting, confused, and uncertain ways to be knowledge-yielding. We must admit a great deal of variability in this area of experience, but I think it can be accounted for on our view just as easily, if not more so, than on the causal theory, for in the causal realm regularities and uniformities are more expected than in the domain of knowledge-yielding experience and thought.

A factor which should not be ignored is that value requirements, according to the position I am urging, are fact-dependent and therefore contextual in nature. The context in which a value requirement holds may be quite complex and thus not often duplicated. This makes for what looks like value relativism. It does indeed make values relative to a given kind of context, but this in no way undermines the objectivity of values. In fact, when we consider the variations in the situations in which people find themselves, the differences in their value experiences and judgments do not at all seem to be so devastating for the claim that such experiences are epistemic.

Furthermore, wherever there are seemings or appearances of things, and this is the case in all realms of epistemic experience, there is a great deal of variability and confusion. In fact, for centuries rationalists regarded our sensory experiences to be too fluctuating and uncertain to be a basis for genuine knowledge. Rational appraisal of experience, however, uses just this feature of it, its inherent inconsistencies, in the search for truth. In fact, without such incompatibilities within experience, there would be no inquiry and no higher levels of thought, for it is precisely this kind of conflict which forces the mind to its higher achievements. With a critical method of assessing the conflicts of sensory experiences and a highly developed theoretical structure within which to operate, sensory experience has become highly reliable within scientific inquiry. Perhaps our emotive and conative experiences would not seem so variable and confused from within a highly critical method of assessing them and a theoretical framework which supported and guided them in the manner scientific method and theory are related to sensory experiences.

Here, I think, is one of the great weaknesses of our culture. The modern mind, for the most part, has no viable theoretical framework to give meaning, direction, and intelligibility to our emotions, passions, joys, sorrows, fears, and longings. Theology at its best attempts to do just this, but theology today is largely discredited as an intellectual discipline.

If value experiences are epistemic, then our moral appraisals may reveal an objectively valid concept of man that embodies an imperative that defines a way of life, for the concept would be embodied in our corroborated and confirmed moral approvals and disapprovals of human behavior, our confirmed moral admiration and contempt of people, and the like.

We must not, however, expect to find in such a normative concept of man a specific blueprint for life. What we find is more like a set of constitutional principles prescribing how a man is to reach decisions about what to become and what to do in various contexts. One who is trained and prepared to function well in any situation, according to the constitutional principles that define the office of a person, is the virtuous and wise man.

Moral virtue, as Aristotle maintained, is the constitution of a person, involving his emotions, which enables him to reach sound judgments about basic values, the ends of conduct. It is somewhat like a scientific mind. To be a scientist, to have a scientific mind, is not simply a matter of knowing scientific truths. We don't educate a man to be a scientist by simply teaching him acquired scientific knowledge. He has to be *trained* to think scientifically. This includes how to formulate and to ask questions, how to observe, what to look for, what constitutes evidence and sound reasoning, the limits of possible solutions, the criteria of an acceptable answer, the creative ability for novel thoughts, etc. All of this comes, if at all, through training and practice. It is a characteristic of the mind which enables one to discover scientific truths. What is the test of whether one thinks scientifically? Can we do any better than to say that one thinks scientifically if one thinks the way a scientist thinks? What is the correct scientific answer to a problem? Can we do any better than to say that it is the answer which the scientist gives, namely, the answer yielded by scientific inquiry? We can say parallel things about moral virtue. It is, I suggest, a condition of mind, a set of habits concerning emotions, attitudes, enjoyments and sufferings, desires and wishes, and thought pertaining to them, produced by training and practice, which enables us to correctly judge, to obtain the truth about, what is good and what is bad, what ought to be and what ought not to be, and thus to correctly set the ends of conduct and, if adequate factual knowledge is available, to choose the right means. The correct solution to a moral problem is what a good and wise man would find to be the solution—the answer found by the exercise of the faculties of an informed, morally virtuous person.

We cannot make sound moral and practical judgments and decisions without fully comprehending and understanding the context in which we live. If our analysis of value judgments is correct, such judgments are always context-dependent. Although some judgments and decisions may be made with regard to only a limited context, some of our basic concerns require a comprehension and understanding of man and his place in reality. Thus all of man's epistemic powers must be brought into play in realizing the image of man revealed in an analysis of moral appraisals.

To be a man, then, is to have a position, an office, defined by certain powers and constitutional principles, the logical grammar of the mind, concerning how these powers are to operate in determining the life to be lived and the living of it. By the nature or concept of man we may say that one is under an imperative to exercise, to develop, to refine, and to critically assess all possible dimensions of experience and thought, learning all that he can from the experience and thought of others in order to comprehend and to understand himself and his world, to discover what he ought to become and ought to do, and to live successfuly, to live a fulfilling, satisfying, meaningful life.

A liberal educational program guided by this image of man could be our chief agency for correcting the derangements and ills of our society and culture, and indeed the major institution for achieving the objectives of our reconstructed civilization. "Our thinking about the aims of education," John W. Gardner, former Secretary of Health, Education, and Welfare, said, "has too often been shallow, constricted and lacking in reach or perspective. Our educational purposes must be seen in the broader framework of our convictions concerning the worth of the individual and the importance of individual fulfillment. . . . We propose that the American people accept as a universal task the fostering of individual development within a framework of rational and moral values. . . . If we accept this concern for individual fulfillment as an authentic national preoccupation, the schools and colleges will then be the heart of a national endeavor. . . . The schools and colleges will be greatly strengthened if their task is undergirded by such a powerful public conception of the goal to be sought." (*Excellence: Can We Be Equal and Excellent Too?* (New York: Harper and Row [Harper Colophon Books], pp. 141-143.)

4

Discrimination and Education

ANTHONY NEMETZ

THE term discrimination by its usage in recent decades has acquired an almost exclusively pejorative connotation. To discriminate now implies acting unfairly, unjustly, or immorally. Very frequently the word *against* accompanies the verb, and the objects of discrimination are most often racial or religious minorities.

Although I cannot gainsay the rule that usage is the ultimate arbiter of correctness, I do want to point out that current usage has obscured a meaning for discrimination which implied approval and commendation. For example, we once praised a man for his discriminating eye or taste. Such usage was, of course, metaphorical, for what was literally intended was to commend a man for his ability to acutely discern, to prudently divide, and to wisely separate. To possess acumen, prudence, and wisdom is hardly cause for censure. On the contrary, the acquisition of such dispositions and habits might well form an epigrammatic statement of educational purposes and goals. It may simply be one of my antiquarian conceits, but I would still like to applaud the man of discrimination, and to commend those educational programs, practices, and principles which enhance the probability of his emergence. And that is precisely what I intend to attempt—to examine in topical fashion some of the more visible places of argument which surround my stated ideals of higher education. My task, then, is itself one of discrimination, i.e., to mark off the distance if any between the ongoing and received practices from the principles requisite for the more facile attainment of achievable goals.

Aristotle long ago noted that it is the mark of wisdom and a fortiori of the wise man to rule or to command. Aristotle's immediate purpose was to describe analogically metaphysics as an architectonic discipline, and he did so by focusing on the most idiomatic feature of a wise man, autonomy. The wise man rules himself, and he evidences self rule by being able to solve difficult problems. I suppose that it is a truism to note that a difficult problem is one which most men cannot solve. And it is platitudinous to observe that the solution to a difficult problem will almost of necessity be apart from or opposed to the conventional wisdom of the day. These observations seem innocent enough, but only superficially so. For what is implied is that if we hope that students are to become wise, they must be autonomous and genuine autonomy is evidenced in the discovery and espousal of principles which exceed or negate the received tradition in every area of inquiry.

Such invention and discovery when judged by conventional standards are unmistakably deviant. And by deviant I mean literally that the view or principle proposed is novel and creative in the sense that every scientific or artistic breakthrough exceeds the traditional transmission of knowledge or breaks with established dogma.

Admittedly there can be no academic courses in invention or seminars in creativity, or workshops in breakthrough; nevertheless, if wisdom is a goal, the university must itself be an active discipline for deviation. To put the matter in more strident terms, a university must be a school for rebels, which I hasten to add is not equivalent to insisting on seeing the university as a proving ground for social scandal.

If we agree or even suppose for the time that the university should not only tolerate deviant thought, but positively encourage it, we must deal with three immediately adjacent views. How does the university encourage or discourage deviation? Are there any constraining limits on the nature or means of such deviation? Is the present form of university structure conducive to the achievement of such goals?

As I noted earlier, intellectual creativity is not itself a subject matter that can be taught. Instead it seems to me improbable if not impossible to become creative in a given discipline by intensified study within that discipline. I suspect but cannot prove that in addition to the obvious need for indigenous talent, disciplinary creativity results from the analogical juxtaposition of principles from apparently incongruent disciplines. For example, the primitive terms in value theory have their origins in classical economics, and however one estimates the worth of value theory, that judgment is not contingent on a prior judgment regarding the validity of classical economics.

But this account of creativity is more of a digressive guess that it is a legitimate account. For if creativity cannot be taught, then its emergence cannot be programmed but only circumstantially expedited. That means that the environment immediately surrounding disciplinary inquiry is the critical catalytic factor. In the language of John Stuart Mill the university has a "pervasive tone."

The description of a "pervasive tone" requires consideration of policies set by the overreaching institutional organization. But such a description equally demands at least a cursory reflection on the way in which students act and react in response to administrative policies, especially those regulating those activities which I have called adjacent to disciplinary inquiry.

I do not believe that anyone would accuse me of flagrant exaggeration if I said that in national terms the university community is currently exhibiting signs of an uneasiness of mind. More brashly put, there is considerable evidence for holding that there are some genuine unsettlements if not outright unrest. My concern with this phenomenon is not to praise or decry the particular social or political issues which have given rise to the disturbances. Instead I want to propose an explanation which is universal enough to be commensurate with the notion of a "pervasive tone."

If the university hopes that its graduates will be discriminating, it has the obligation of inducting the student into his intellectual patrimony. The university community must have a decent interest in, if not a reverence for, the past. But the only justification for the intellectual transmission of historical achievements is that it serve as a vector and incentive for present critique and hopefully for future creativity. Homer said that we swear by what is ancient, but as his first commentators noted, we can also swear at it. The past must indeed be read, but it is doubtful that it ought to be studied as past. For to study the past as past makes the student as well as the teacher archeological taxonomists, or worse cultish curators of dessication. Such perverse preoccupation with the past has two obvious and untoward consequences. In the first place it creates a tone which at least effectively inhibits desired deviation, and at most proscribes the emergence of the autonomous man.

The second consequence is contingent upon the university completely misunderstanding its function. And it exhibits such misunderstanding when it not only canonizes the past, but then goes on to hallow the conditions, virtues, and customs of the past as rigidly normative for the present.

If the university accepts programatically either or both of these two misuses of history, alma mater simply becomes a fallen woman. Instances of both kinds of misuse are unfortunately easy to discover. As a spectacularly extreme instance of the misuse of history I cite the efforts of the Mississippi legislature not only to write history, but to write a history of something which did not and could not have happened. For example, the official textbook explanation of the Civil War is in outline stated as follows. The War of Yankee Aggression was caused by crop failure in the North which in turn was caused by Yankees following the English style of farming and, as everyone knows, where there are no trees nothing grows. A second and more recent example is the claim that the federal government is eroding, grasping, snatching, expropriating, robbing, despoiling or perhaps taking away the holy of holies—States' Rights. But a quick glance at the Constitution of the Confederacy reveals that "our way" of political life was not always so conceived. In fact Article VI of the Confederate Constitution has the identical wording of the X Amendment of the U. S. Constitution, and the establishment of a Supreme Court together with a specification of its powers is also identical in both constitutions.

As I noted these examples were really exercises in thinking about the impossible, and as such are extreme. The most common form of concretizing history—one which is not regionally idiosyncratic—is the worrisome watching by administration, alumni, and concerned citizenry lest an unseemly tone pervade the campus. And apparently the most objectionable tone conceivable to some is one which denies that the university ought to be a ghetto, albeit a disciplinary one, and equally denies that membership in the university community imposes special obligations of concern for and involvement in the community at large.

The rhetoric for defending the ghetto syndrome is familiar enough. "The business of the student is to learn, and the business of the teacher is to teach. And let those in charge of the social and political communities—men of practical knowledge and experience—run the community." The assertion that teaching and learning are proper functions of the university is valid on its face. But the denial that the university has an especial obligation for social and political involvement has consequences which I find intolerable.

Before spelling out those untoward entailments, I want to admit that I have assumed and in no way proved that the university has the especial obligations I have claimed for it. I feel certain that a historical survey of the charters and chartularia of universities from the middle ages on would substantiate that claim. But for this paper I will rest on showing what happens if the claim is denied.

To limit the proper functions of the university to narrowly defined academic pursuits is in legal terms an effective deterrent. To continue the legal analogy, imprisonment and indeed execution are often justified as a deterrent to any contemplated anti-social behavior. Seen in this way, the concept of deterrence is a viable way of securing social conformity. The notion of social conformity has at least two discernible dimensions—action and thought. Criminal law is charged with imposing remedies on socially undesirable behavior, i.e., behavior which does not conform to the ethical and moral norms of the society. And I can find no fault in the principle that society should legislate against behavior that is socially destructive. But, of course, that in no way implies that every such legislative enactment of judicial decision is just.

Having said that deterrence is a plausible legal defense for securing that amount of conformity of action which insures the security of the society, I now categorically deny the appropriateness of that line of argument for the conduct of academe. And the constriction of the functions of the university to teaching and learning under the sanction of concretized history is precisely a deterrent to the invention, discovery, and espousal of such deviant thought without which society can neither progress nor survive. For without deviant thought there will be no discriminating men to lead the society.

I am fully aware that many an administrative panjandrum will judge these reflections innocuously vacuous. After all, any number of universities have citizenship in their mottoes, social science in their curricula, and service as a part of their statutory functions. I have no intention of denying the obvious, but I do assert that such a reduced inventory is by no means the full stock of a pervasive tone.

Campus interests and activities seem to be the most reliable indices to the pervasive tone. I refer again in the broadest sense to the totality of extra-curricular activities of the campus, both for faculty and students, and the ways in which those activities are monitored, supervised, and regulated. The regulations governing extra-curricular activities are in every instance decidedly a revelation of administrative social expectations, but are equally an index of the intellectual aspirations of the community. I am totally persuaded that what is allowed and expected outside the classroom profoundly affects classroom performance on both sides of the lectern.

Again allow me to turn to my legal analogy. The enactment of criminal law is not only a punitive response to violations against anti-social behavior, it equally reflects societal expectations of what kind of behavior will be socially acceptable. And the rules and regulations which govern extra-curricular activity can and do serve not only as a deterrent to unacceptable behavior, but may indeed be a prospective deterrent with the result that specific norms of conformity are easily evidenced by legislated codes of conduct.

If my argument has any merit to this point, I am forced into an uncomfortable position. For I have argued that one of the overarching goals of the university is intellectual deviation. I have also insisted that extra-curricular attitudes and activities largely influence curricular performance and success. Consequently, if the university is to foster deviant thought, it must also allow and promote deviant behavior at least to the extent that extra-curricular activity influences disciplinary inquiry.

It is reasonable to expect that this last claim will be clarified. In doing so, I want once again to discriminate between ongoing practices and desirable programs. Most major universities have some form of student government, honor codes, student handbooks, which specify both substantive and procedural rules for dealing with unacceptable behavior. On legal grounds I cannot fault the practice of establishing and enforcing rules. In recent years the courts have clearly stated that universities may make rules governing student behavior as long as such rules serve educational purposes. But it surely is not the function of the courts to define educational purposes. A judicial determination of educational purposes would be totalitarian, and the absence of all rules is anarchical. Both situations are intolerable, for they equally deny the required freedom intrinsic to shared inquiry.

The real issue, then, is not whether there are to be rules but what kind of educational purposes are presupposed or furthered by the rules, and, secondly, who is charged with the formulation and execution of rules.

I have no intention of discussing particular rules such as curfew because judgment about the validity or propriety of a given rule depends on the undefined notion of educational purpose. Instead, allow me to make some personal reflections on the current systems of rules. The observations will be general and largely undefined, but I think I could make a reasonable argument for each.

I am opposed on moral and intellectual grounds to honor codes and to every extension of rules justified by "in loco parentis" with its accompanying set of parietals and grand-parietals. My reason is straightforward. All such codes and rules are more or less fanciful ways of perpetuating the Protestant ethic (in Weber's sense of the term) as the norm of acceptable behavior. It is an ethic of individualism, economic in tenor, traditional in perspective, and socially disinterested in outlook. Its product, if not its intent, is to produce an entrepreneural conformist who is commodiously corporate. And I object to that as relevant to educational purposes precisely because the public interest of our society especially in its social dimensions cannot be furthered by social disinterestedness even when qualified by personal philanthropy and governmental support and directive.

The stubborn retention of the Protestant ethic as an extra-curricular norm of behavior in the second kind of misused or concretized history which is anachronistic and, therefore, procrustean. It enforces or reinforces the ghetto mind by successfully truncating social concern and involvement. The immediately educational effect of such amputation is to intensify an intellectual attitude which is content with historical transmission, and which is totally innocent of the needed relation of relevance between the affairs of academe and the work of society. It inhibits the shared "adventure in ideas," and substitutes for that ideal an acquisitive attitude for knowledge with all the attendant preoccupation of a corporation concerned with production, profit, and a successful way of phasing out losers.

I think the same point can be articulated by viewing the national student unrest in terms that are more idiomatic to the students. This generation has learned to "cope," and is practiced in "doing somebody else's thing." But not doing one's own thing is being given a "bad bag," and faced without an alternative, the answer is to "opt out"—the birth of a "hippie." I am not interested here in debates about tonsorial inelegance, flower power or impotence, not even with misunderstood Zen, or contacts with the numinous associated with a "grass party" or an "acid blast." Most if not all of these practices constitute a self-conscious effrontery calculated only to buff the chrome plated self righteousness of people over thirty. The uniform and the liturgy of dissatisfaction will pass, but, if present codes and procedures remain, not the unrest which it evidences. For seen in the light of students, if "hippie" connotes "opting out" of today's society—a society that simply must devise solutions to international and national problems which threaten life more than an assumedly inherited way of life—then it is the university who is the real "hippie." I am now referring not to the university as administration, but to the whole academic community. For example, a recently popular song advised us to "listen to what the children say, when they play skip a rope." And one would be just as well advised to watch out and listen on a Monday night, when a sorority emerges from its cloistered security, assembles out front chastely garbed in virginal white and with monastic solemnity chants its hopeful hymeneal hymns. Who is the real "hippie"? Who has "opted out"?

The problem of unrest as I understand it goes far beyond the maintenance or defiance of particular institutionalized practices. Who can afford the luxury of becoming exercised about uniforms, when indefensible terrorism becomes the standard preamble to negotiating differences? Anarchy is at least as destructive of educational purposes as is any conceivable set of arbitrary parietals. I cannot defend or applaud a course of truculent unreasonableness no matter who initiates it, and recent events have shown that unreasonableness is not held in fee simply by administrators. And the current mood of the governing community, including the U. S. Congress, is not only one of disappointment and anger, but of retribution that seems inordinately vindictive. Proposed legislation seems to say that the failing of a system of prospective deterrence will find a remedy in a radical retribution. I for one cannot believe that educational purposes can be furthered this way. Nor, indeed, is total permissiveness any more viable a solution than recurrent repression. What, then, shall be the limit on deviant behavior, for on legal, moral, and educational grounds, some assignable limit must be found—a limit which is not so much a restraining order as it is an injunction to facilitate the achievement of educational goals.

Recently the U. S. Commissioner of Education opined that the faculty was primarily responsible for the irresponsible forms of student protest. I somewhat grudgingly suspect that he is correct, at least to the extent that if the faculty are obligated to encourage deviant behavior, they are equally responsible for at least proposing a limit on the tolerable forms of such behavior. I, therefore, will attempt to make such a proposal, but to do it by considering three aspects of disciplinary concern. My expectation is the converse of an earlier assumption in which I asserted that extra-curricular activities profoundly affect curricular effort. Hence if we reconsider some adjustments or reforms that are narrowly academic, it may well reveal a direction to the solution of the extracurricular problem.

The first of my concerns turns on the priority of loyalties to which the professor of today subscribes. The profession and not the particular university in which he works commands his highest allegiance, and within the teaching profession, the disciplinary peer group, the professional associations, also commands more loyalty than the university at which he is presently based. The reason for this arrangement of priorities is easier to explain than to justify. A man wants his work fairly evaluated and in the widest possible context. And a particular university context, no matter how large, can only partially accomplish this because of the proliferation of special competencies.

The simple fact of this order of priorities makes the present administrative structure of most universities ineffectual with respect to the judgment of man's work, and in many cases a hindrance if not an overt threat to the achievement of educational goals. The familiar structure of a university into colleges and/or divisions was a response to a theory of knowledge which divided intellectual labors. That structure implied that the administrative head of a particular area was himself a knowledgeable member of a disciplinary peer group. I know of no one today who still holds the theory of knowledge which gave rise to our present administrative structure. Consequently, present administrative structure simply cannot be responsive to disciplinary advances and could hardly be expected to be responsible for educational innovation. The concept of a college or division is no longer viable. It is a monument to nostalgia which impedes change and impairs progress. This indictment of the structure is by no means to be understood as an invective directed against the holders of administrative office. A goodly number of administrators were and are most reluctant to take the office because they are neither trained nor inclined to become archivists, data synopsizers, and crypto statisticians. There are, of course, proposals suggesting that what is now needed in college administrative posts are not men with scholarly backgrounds, but a specially trained managerial class. I reject that suggestion because all that would accomplish is to do more efficiently what is already useless. I simply see no alternative to a radical reformation of the administrative structure for an additional reason.

The priorities of loyalties I mentioned, together with the ineffective administrative structure, have produced a serious deterioration of faculty-student relations. For the sake of requirements, most often more democratically than educationally arrived at, and for the sake of accurately recording such formal misadventures, teachers have assumed a new role. In the language of the Western movie, we have become drovers herding the cattle down the old I.B.M. trail, being careful not to lose any strays in card-punch canyon, in point hour gulch or in upper divisional flats. And we do this under the goad of the ramrod—the dean—who in turn is given orders by the trail-boss—the registrar or the keeper of the machine.

Not only are we making concessions to poor academic practice, but the same factors have led us to tolerate in other departments and divisions what is intolerable in our own discipline—the Mickey Mouse course. To be sure it can only happen in other departments, but then courtesy demands the possibility of the reciprocity of charge. In short, a revamping of administrative structure is required to provide the faculty with the means for effective self-policing of matters strictly academic. As I see it, or guess at it, administrative reorganization in light of current disciplinary practices might well result in emphasizing functions that are now incidentally dealt with or accidentally touched upon. For example, the office of academic dean could become that of coordinator both of interdepartmental programs and faculty that service such programs. The office of dean could be that of curricular review and especially experimentation. Preoccupation with budget need not continue. If we have a faculty committee on curriculum and tenure, is there a plausible reason for not having a faculty committee on budgets which could review the various departmental requests? With such emphasis the administrators would have released time to become concerned with and directly involved in the society which is the subject of scientific inquiry of a wide variety. Thus, a possible byproduct of administrative reorganization would be the more direct involvement of the university in the surrounding society, the present lack of which is evidently one of the sources of student unrest.

The second of the academic concerns to which I want to call attention is the extreme mobility of the faculty. It has become fashionable not only for departments to compete for individual top talent, but for universities to buy entire established departments. Group or team movement is becoming common-place, and the reputation of a university, like our technological environment, is instant. Such mobility is clearly in the self interest of the teacher, and it would be unseemly of me to denigrate rewarding motives. Despite the possible personal rewards that accompany mobility, it does have two oft noted dangers. To get to where the action is, a man must do attention-getting work. This means grantsmanship, more scholarly writing than normal inclination would likely dictate, and continuing professional performances including giving papers at symposia. Time with and for students has a lesser priority than professional advancement. To be sure this is one of the sources of the generation segregation, and another reasonable cause of student unrest as evidenced by the student grievances at Berkeley.

In addition to aggravating the distance between students and faculty, I believe that faculty mobility has other effects which are not in the public interest. Undergraduate students are in the main institutionally bound, and the instructional quality at a given university is an annual variable. In addition there is always the difference between the poor and the endowed, with an unfortunate disparity in the institutional quality of education. As a partial solution to that problem I suggest that conferences or consortiums of universities, such as the S.E.C., programmatically develop a system of exchange which would be an extrapolation of some programs already in existence. For example, some schools do have a junior year abroad, and others have exchange scholar programs at the graduate level. What I would propose is that undergraduate students, individually or in groups upon faculty advice, be encouraged to study for a quarter, semester, or year with men on the campuses of cooperating institutions, of course without tuition penalty.

The purpose of this proposal would be to make the student body or parts of it as mobile as the faculty, and in that way enhance the quality of educational experience. (For the sake of the alumni, I would not extend this program to football players.) It might also be possible to design a system of faculty exchange with cooperating institutions—a kind of academic VISTA program with the more wealthy sharing with their less privileged brethren. But this would be more difficult than creating patterns of student mobility.

The scheme of professional priorities has not only led to a growing disengagement of faculty direction of students, but also has predictably occasioned the incredible growth, power, and influence of non-curricular university agencies. I refer of course to counseling, guidance, and deans of students. As in the case of administrators, I do not fault them individually or corporately. Their succession to power could not have been accomplished without faculty abdication. I believe them when they say they are concerned with the education of the students as much as the faculty. Unfortunately for the faculty, the orientation of the non-curricular university agencies cannot in the nature of the case be identical with that of the faculty. The vested and overcoated interests of public officials, alumni, image conscious administrators, especially in publicly supported institutions, make a cogent argument for norms of behavior that are in most cases contrary to the educational aspirations of the faculty.

The result is obvious. Students who as high school teenagers had an apparent social, especially economic function in society, come to the university where they and their lives are absolutely *quasi*. Their parents are replaced by rules, their sense of the future shrouded by the past, their sense of duty emasculated by the rhetoric of privilege which demands gratitude rather than commitment. At orientations they are hailed as leaders of the future, and then asked to behave as followers of the past. They are encouraged to play at democracy, but reprimanded for trying to improve society. As a cartoonist put it, they are taught to think for themselves and violently upbraided if they learn well. What else could result from all this but a socially ineffective group which when it discovers it is ineffectual by design becomes restless and resentful. What surprises me is not that students are protesting but that it has taken so long to do so.

But having said all that, I still am obligated to do more than welcome extra-curricular deviant behavior. The limit which I want to set is, I think, genuinely contained in my three concerns resulting from the schema of faculty loyalties. I do not believe that a permanent workable norm can be found or negotiated within the university as it now exists. To be sure, temporary solutions can be invoked which may range from police force to court settlement. But all such settlements are made under the assumption that the roles of the existing structure of the university—administration, faculty, and auxiliary services—are adequate for the present and viable for the future. And this I deny.

If the university of today is successfully to discharge its unique obligation to society, it must reverse the trend of the last quarter of a century and insist that the totality of disciplinary goals set the tone for all extra-curricular rules, codes, and procedures. And that categorically means that the *teaching* staff not only define educational goals, but must be empowered to implement them. What I am suggesting is not the protest of the academic proletariat, scheming to become an imperial elite. For my part, I, like the protesting students, simply want to do my thing, and I cannot do it if a goodly portion of my time is spent in researching ways of beating the system and negotiating with the establishment.

Let's have it and done with it. The university is both of and in the society. That means that students like all other citizens are fully liable to civil and criminal law which is societally administered and enforced. Protective custody is not a reasonable means of encouraging maturity of thought and action.

However, I do admit that the academic community is not totally of and in the community. And the sense in which it is different is the supposedly unique relation of teacher and student as well as the interrelations of the students themselves. To the end of fully realizing the possibilities inherent in the student-teacher relation, I have called for administrative reorganization. As an integral part of such reorganization I would insist that the student be directly liable to the judgment of teaching staff and not to computerized decisions. Academic suspension and dismissal ought not to be mechanically determined but prudentially decided. And by the same token, academic probation could be imposed on students for not working at their full capacities rather than for performing below statistical norms. Such discretionary responsibility is already exercised at the graduate level. Why should undergraduates be deprived of such concern? To the possible objection that we simply would not have the time, nor would the majority of students welcome that kind of direction, I can only say that we already have dual track education, regular and honors, and all I am insisting upon is that we have a dual system of sanction and responsibility.

Throughout this paper I have argued that the realization of academic goals depends upon the pervasive tone of the university. That tone was optimally characterized as the encouragement of deviant behavior, but that limits on the level of tolerance of such deviant behavior must be made. I have pointed to the legal and the narrowly academic limits. Now a final suggestion on the intra-mural limit of deviant behavior. If students are to become wise and prudent, they must become practiced in those mutual responsibilities that make community living rewarding rather than barely tolerable. And the level of community living cannot be coextensive with the total university. Given the irreducible pluralism of temperament and conviction, I think it self defeating to impose a uniform code on all. Instead I can see no reason why such rules could not effectively be self-determining on an individual housing unit basis, so as to give the individual student the greatest possible latitude not only in determining under what rules he would live, but also in whose company he would make and keep them. To a large extent this is already the case for fraternities and I am egalitarian enough to abolish the distinction between Greek and Spartan.

Under such changed conditions I think the student would be more likely to discern an appropriately personal educational end, divide the instructionally meaningful from the meaningless, and separate the socially significant from the irrelevant. He would in short become the discriminating man, whom I want to applaud.

5

Rights of Youth

HENRY DAVID AIKEN

WE live in a time of monumental paradoxes. When they occur in
the mathematical and natural sciences, paradoxes represent a
breakdown in thought only. But when they occur in the social or
political, the moral or religious spheres, where by definition thinking concerns our existence as human beings, they can become mor-
tally dangerous. However, paradoxes wear two faces: one a face of
puzzlement, confusion, defeat or despair; the other of fascination,
challenge, opportunity. The most stunning breakthroughs, whether
in the sciences, in philosophy, or in social and psychological
thought, occur when someone discovers a new technique, invents a
new tool, achieves a new perspective which by enabling us to see
around a paradox makes is possible for us both to have our cake
and eat it. Then we no longer need strive merely to shore up our
ruins. Even tragedy is redeemed when we convert it into art. Now
for the time being, we are once more out in the blue, and so having
given form to chaos, we can press on to new reaches of human
possibility.

Some of the contemporary paradoxes I have called human or
existential may be witnessed (the selection is virtually at random)
in the so-called "death of God" movement in religion, in the new
moralities which at first look seem merely new forms of immorality
or amorality, in the cult of anti-art, in the resistance and civil disobedience movements, in various student revolt movements which
appear to threaten the very conditions of student existence.

This last paradox, which might be called alternatively, "the paradox of the student" or "the paradox of the university," is but one
of a complex of "paradoxes of youth" or again alternatively, "paradoxes of maturity." In this essay I shall suggest some ways of
coping with those which confront us all in our thinking about rights
and responsibilities of young people in an age in which many youths
view themselves virtually as a race apart while at the same time demanding immediate entrance into the ranks of adult citizens. On
this score, the young people's position is merely a counter-image of
elders. We—and here I include many who still seek to preserve
identity with a tradition that calls itself liberal and democratic—

61

subject our youth to a permanent Selective Service about whose existence, standards of selection, or uses youth has little or nothing to say. Our economic and educational systems undoubtedly offer extraordinary opportunities for rapid advancement at least to well-off or gifted young men and women. For example, youths who have not cut their wisdom teeth are offered full professorships or placed in charge of research projects demanding the most intricate skills and the subtlest forms of understanding. Yet our legal and political systems still treat them as minors or semi-majors who cannot vote or else are unable to hold public office. Beyond all this our affluent society has fathered an affluent youth free to do and to possess many things of which a half century ago even the most extravagant member of the leisure class did not dream. Yet in matters of political judgment and social responsibility we treat them, especially in crucial situations, as children.

II

Now political, social, and moral attiutudes are always corre-lated, directly or indirectly, with conceptions of human nature. Before going on to develop a new theory about rights of youth, we must therefore ask whether certain traditional ideas about human development do not stand in need of revision. The classical view, inherited with little modification from the Greeks, is that man's nature is largely fixed, and that as in the case of all other natural kinds there is a certain mature human character which every un-thwarted human being seeks to actualize. About a half century ago, a fascinating inversion of this theory, identified largely with the name of Freud, began to take its place. According to this view (vastly over-simplified), the fundamental psychological problems of adult life are set in infancy or early childhood. From the moment he is thrust into the world, each individual is subject to certain characteristic traumas, complexes, forms of repression and compulsory release or compensation which largely govern his behavior for the rest of his life. And liberation comes, for a very few, through a lengthy and usually costly process of analysis, devoted to uncovering archetypal forms of maladjustment, based on the same infantile traumas and complexes.

Here it is unnecessary to dwell upon the overwhelming preoccupation with the sexual drive and its misadventures in this psychology or its oversimplified conception of the mature human personality. Instead, let us look at some more recent ideas which provide bases for a more subtly differentiated account of the phases of human development, according to which the child is to be viewed neither as father to the man, nor as the man in embryo, but on the contrary each child, like the aging individual that will one day replace it, is in certain respects a creature unto itself. In particular, I have in mind the work of psychologists such as Erik Erikson (who, significantly, came to his work as a psychoanalyst after a career as an artist) who now talk very compellingly about a number of distinct life-stages, each with its own qualities of being, its distinct forms of creativity and sterility, its corresponding fulfillments and failures, its characteristic crises and ways of coping with them. From this point of view, none of us is a single, developing person, but rather a sequence of related persons. In an important sense, two adolescents may in fact have a closer, more intimate identity with each other than either has with the strange oldster that will one day bear his name.

My own interest is in a conception of youth which overlaps but does not exactly coincide with Erikson's notion of the life stage of adolescence. Yet much that he has to say about adolescents as "transitory existentialists by nature because they become suddenly capable of realizing a separate identity" has direct bearing upon the ideas I have come to in developing a new theory about rights of youth. The conception of youth I have in mind also overlaps the next stage in Erikson's "epigenetic cycle," which he calls "young adulthood." At this stage the individual youth, having made a start in coping with his problems of personal identity, now moves on to issues created by interpersonal relationships, particularly such ones as friendship, love, and sexual intimacy. But this is also a time when the crisis of identity, as Erikson calls it, partly resolves itself in the form of a special sense of "intimacy with oneself, one's inner resources, the range of one's excitements and commitments." And just as the adolescent, actively seeking his own identity is subject to special problems concerning the social roles he is expected to play, which he often resolves through some sort of generalized religious or ideological conversion, through identification with some larger presence to which he can give his loyalty, so the young adult becomes involved in distinctive problems of isolation which he tries to resolve, for example, through marriage and, according to his talents and interests, through some form of dedicated work. The period of adolescence and young manhood is thus a time both of passionate searching for independence and of striving for ideal attachments and forms of unselfish achievement.

Much of this spells out what we already know intuitively. Who can fail to perceive the extraordinary precocity, the energy, and capacity for sympathetic involvement in great (as well as less great) "causes" which are so characteristic of human beings in this marvelous springtime of life? And who can be unaware of the special forms of vulnerability, the yearning, restlessness, loneliness, and unspeakable unhappiness to which young people are liable?

It would appear that if thinkers like Erikson are even half right, we must question all approaches to problems concerning rights and responsibilities of youths, inbred in us since the time of the Greek philosophers, which treat youth as merely a potential something else and the time of youth as merely a bridge-passage between childhood and manhood. Every period of life, if it comes to that, is a time of transition, and this is no less true of the householder of fifty than of his youthful children. A youth is already something, with a form and an identity of his own. And if, from one point of view, he is not fully mature, the same can as well be said from another viewpoint of the man "at the (supposed) height of his powers" who has yet not attained to that distinctive ripeness and wisdom of life one finds in the works of such incomparable, self-rejuvenating old men as Dewey and Russell and Freud, as Verdi and Stravinsky and Yeats, or as Tillich and Martin Buber. Indeed, the very word "rejuvenate" itself suggests that in restructuring our thinking about the problems of youth, and the rights pertaining thereto, we may find clues to a reconstruction of our attitudes toward the problems of later phases of the human life cycle, and so discover good reasons to modify uninflected and uniformitarian doctrines about the rights of man which we have inherited, like pieces of old furniture, from another era when the pressing needs of men in societies created problems of equality and fraternity, as well as liberty, in many ways quite different from our own.

III

Our problems about rights of youth would remain formidable even with the help of the best available psychological theories about this extraordinary period of life. Unfortunately, the very terms in which the topic is discussed—youth, adulthood, maturity, above all rights—are subject to misconceptions that cause us to falter in the very act of thinking about them. Moreover, these are not terms employed in sorting out natural objects that help us to play a neutral animal, vegetable, and mineral game with members of the human race. Through them, on the contrary, we contemplate roles, assign functions, and make decisions central to all political, social, and moral life. How can we answer one of the great and pressing questions of our age, whether youths should share the rights of adults, if because of misconceptions and preconceptions about what a right, a youth, or an adult is, we cannot clearly envision the possibilities which the question demands us to consider? I fear that nothing can be done until we refurbish some parts of the conceptual apparatus with which we must work.

Our notions about the concept of a right are perhaps the most confused. By this time moral philosophers have succeeded in removing a part of the accumulated dust that overlays our conceptions of good and evil and moral right and wrong. Legal and political philosophers are making progress with such terms as law, authority, revolution and, ideology. But the elusive concept of a right, which has such important applications in every sphere of human action is covered with a dozen coats of ideological varnish which are nearly impossible to remove.

For example, since the advent of utilitarianism and pragmatism in the 19th century, influential thinkers everywhere have tended to conflate the ideas of a right and a good. This error is egregious. Granted that many, though by no means all, rights are among our most precious political or human values, there are many goods to which we can claim no right at all. The task of a doctrine of rights is to specify, and hence to restrict, those goods to which we can meaningfully regard ourselves as entitled. That is why a true bill of rights is of such immense importance to a society. For only after making sure that no relevant rights would be seriously infringed can we consider whether a good can be justly pursued. The "pragmatic theory" of rights, as I shall call it, encourages its advocates, governmental officials as well as private citizens, to treat rights as merely one set of values among many which therefore may be thrown indiscriminately into the pot of deliberation where prospective policies are cooked. This is its overwhelming fault. For it returns us, in effect, to a Hobbesian state of nature where the liberties of each man, subject to no constraining bills of entitlement, are unlimited.

I am not suggesting that it is never proper to abridge or alter rights. But anyone who would do so has his work cut out for him. For it is the abridgment, not the right, that needs justification, and the good achieved by abridging or abandoning it must be at once overwhelming and at least as palpable as the right in question. This is why many young people, often conservative in their basic attitudes toward the American system, are moved to rebellion by pragmatic political and military policies which, in the name of an impalpable something called "the national interest," ride roughshod over their rights both as youths and as young citizens of a supposedly liberal-democracy. It is also why black men, not ill-disposed to the principles of a free society, are maddened by pragmatic realists who calmly ask them to wait indefinitely for substantive enjoyment of their rights until the cold war has been won, until the city planners have cleared the slums, or the political parties have been made responsive to something other than their own interests.

Two other misconceptions are worth mentioning, for they are also prevailing sources of confused thinking and acting. One is the "gift theory" of rights. According to it, rights are happy benefits bestowed upon us by some beneficent person or institution: a relative, God, the state, the university. This will not do. All of us, I trust, are grateful for the gifts we receive from known or unknown donors. But if we respond rationally we do not on that account claim them as rights. No right is violated when a gift is not forthcoming. Among the ancient Hebrews, men were held to enjoy certain rights, which God himself is bound to respect, in virtue of a covenant made between Him and his people. That covenant in fact was taken as proof that God is a responsible person, not simply an all-powerful Santa Claus. The trouble with the gift theory, as we shall see more clearly presently, is that it ignores the correlative notion of responsibility, without which the concept of a right is meaningless. One of the things we perceive intuitively to be wrong with even the most benevolent of dictators is that the privileges they bestow are merely gifts. For what is given according to one's pleasure may be withheld for the same reason. Those radicals who profess to despise liberalism would do well to ponder the fact that one of the immense strengths of the liberal tradition of John Locke and his followers among our own revolutionary founding fathers was their grasp of the confusions implicit in the gift theory of rights.

But now we have to consider, all too briefly, another theory which, while it contains much truth, still does not provide an adequate general conception of rights. This is the "juristic" or "legalist" theory which holds that, following the model of the law, a right is to be understood as a recognized social practice. From this point of view, for example, the right to be at liberty amounts in fact to a system of social or legal permissions which a society or its government recognizes and for violations of which it provides acknowledged remedies. Accordingly this theory advances a great step beyond those previously considered. For by implication it clearly recognizes that when a person has a right then some other person or persons have a responsibility to observe or protect it. Furthermore, legal rights are forms of practice determined by the rules of a legal-political system. In this connection it should be remarked that another merit of the classical liberal tradition is contained in its insistence that sound government, which includes an acceptable system of law, must have as its first objective the establishment of a

set of such practices in the form of a constitutional bill of rights
that limits the spheres of public as well as private action.

Two other merits of the juristic theory deserve mention; one concerning the concept of a law, and hence by implication that
of a legal right; the other, at least in its contemporary forms,
concerning its view of the general relation of law to morality.
As to the first point, because the juristic theory contends that
a law as such cannot be fully understood as "a command of a
sovereign," as realist utilitarians and pragmatists have contended,
but only as a rule tied umbilically to a general rule of law to
which any rightful sovereign is also subject, it helps to protect
us from undiscriminating forms of cynicism, to which young people
in our time seem particularly prone, which treat legal rights
as nothing more than *de facto* permissions of those who hold power.

I am not unmindful here that existing legal systems are very
imperfect approximations to a true rule of law. Every black
man, every migrant worker, and many, many youths have learned
to their sorrow that our own legal system is full of unpardonable
lapses from the commonest principles of justice inherent in a
rule of law. All the same, to vary a thesis of David Hume, the
first rational act of those driven to overthrow an existing
legal-political system must be to establish another more
equitable, surer, and closer to the principle of a true rule of
law. Nor, important as it is, need we make a sacred cow of the
idea of a rule of law; for no matter how excellent it may be
it does not exhaust what we understand by justice. And justice
is not the only good we require of a politically organized society.
A rule of law, in short, is a necessary but by no means a sufficient
condition of tolerable government or of an acceptable legal system.
For we must ask not only that justice be done but that the
justice done, however impeccable, is adequate in all the spheres
of life which law and government affect.

But this leads directly to the other merit of the juristic theory;
its recognition of the logical distinction between the law as it
is and the law as it should or ought to be. This distinction, which
provides the indispensable leverage for responsible demand for
rightful changes in regard either to particular laws or to the
legal system as a whole, is ignored both by sentimental
exponents of "the law" as the embodiment of a system of ideals,
and by legal realists and pragmatists whose distaste for moralism
spills over into contempt for moral criticism itself. All systems
of law fall well short of what they ought to be, and sentimentalists
do them no service by forever reminding us that "the spirit of the
law" dwelling within them is something just and good. Law and
morality are not the same thing, and the deliberations of a

Solomon become confused when he runs them together.

My purpose, then, is not to raise questions about the need for qualification of the theory of law underlying modern versions of the juristic theory of rights. And for the sake of argument, at least, I am prepared to accept it as a working hypothesis about the law itself in dealing with issues concerning rights of youth that are only in the second instance legal. I contest only the thesis that a legal right, viewed as an established practice within a system of law, affords a suitable model for a general conception of rights, especially those of the sort we call moral or ethical. On the contrary, it turns out in its own way to be prejudicial to a study of rights of youth which, although very real, are not yet embodied in any established social or legal practice.

In the following paragraphs it is possible to give only a bare outline of a general theory of rights for which I have argued elsewhere. First, let me say that in the widest sense a right is not definable as a kind of rule or practice, even though it may afford the basis for establishing a practice. It is entirely meaningful, for example, for one person to say to another, "I grant you the right to make a practice of walking over my land." The right in this case isn't a practice; although it may provide the ground for a practice. Furthermore, it is meaningful to say, "I grant you the right, on this occasion, to walk across my land." This, note well, is no mere gift. For if I grant such a right then in so doing I hold myself responsible either to respect the freedom of him to whom it is granted or, conceivably, to guarantee that he will not be molested either by myself or others when he takes his walk. In short, in granting a right I create a claim whose terms I thereby obligate myself to honor, even though by the terms of the grant it may lapse when a single action has been performed. Thus, whereas a legal right is not merely the basis of a practice or an action, but a practice in its own right which correspondingly imposes a recurrent duty toward those who may claim the right in question, a moral right, on the other hand, exists whenever a claim may be made that some person or other obliges himself to respect, whether or not a practice of any sort exists.

A second feature of significant ascriptions of rights, especially those of the moral sort, is that since they implicitly involve assignments of responsibility, they are never correctly understood simply as statements of fact. It is one thing to say that a young man possesses the abilities for entering college; but it is another to claim that those abilities entitle him to go to college. Statements of fact ask us merely to accept something as the case; ascriptions of rights impose responsibilities and therefore are always intended to dispose those to whom they are addressed to be ready to perform (or refrain from performing) an act or acts of a certain kind when the circumstances warrant. Ascriptions of rights, in short, belong to the domain, not of what philosophers (misleadingly) called theoretical, but of practical reason. And reason functions practically only when it operates, to vary a famous thesis of Karl Marx, not simply to describe reality but to change it.

But here we have reached a place where the liberal tradition is most vulnerable. For, since the time of Locke, that tradition has been concerned largely with rights, whether moral or legal, that pertain only to so-called negative liberties. Such rights permit us to do as we please in certain circumstances—say, save our lives, enjoy and protect our property, or follow our own way to happiness—but permissions entail no primary obligation on the part of others save to refrain from interfering with the actions of those who possess them. If they elect to go to hell in a bucket, we pledge only not to stand in their way. The idealist and socialist traditions, which in this respect go further back behind Locke to the Greeks, remind us that there is more to the rights of civilized life than license to do as we like. Some rights lay claim to what are sometimes called "positive freedoms." These rights are not simply permissions, but on the contrary require all responsible persons actively to aid and support those who possess them. Rights of this sort are of particular importance in the case of young people who even when they already possess powers of judgment and discrimination are commonly without the means of realizing their ends. And it is precisely with respect to rights of this sort that liberals, as John Stuart Mill for one came eventually to see, have had much to learn from the socialist tradition.

Now, as I have indicated, the concept of a right is inescapably correlated with that of responsibility. No one can significantly claim a right unless there is someone who is obliged to honor the claim. Before ascribing rights, therefore, it is essential to inquire who, if anyone, may be held responsible for their observance. And in the case of rights of youth, this point is also of particular importance, since it is commonly, though by no means always true, that those who must assume the primary burden of responsibility no longer enjoy exactly similar rights. Efforts to enlarge or modify rights of youth thus impose great problems of understanding and sympathy, for most of us find it easier to acknowledge another's right when we ourselves also possess it. These problems are further complicated in societies like our own where simplistic uniformitarian doctrines of justice prevail and where, especially in the economic sphere, people are still left so largely to their own inadequate devices. At the theoretical level it is widely taken for granted that if all rights entail responsibilities, then all rights and responsibilities must be mutual. This is plainly false. For example, aged persons have rights which entail no mutual responsibilities. But this is not all. For in principle, rights and responsibilities need not be reciprocal. Insane or senile persons have rights, though virtually by definition they can assume few or no responsibilities. But even when some form of reciprocity is just, it can by no means always be established by appeal to a principle of equality.

In summary, a tenable general theory of rights must make allowance in advance for many possibilities of differential treatment among human beings according to their various circumstances and powers. This does not mean that we should abandon entirely the principles inscribed in doctrines that speak of the rights of man. Nor does it mean that we renounce altogether libertarian doctrines about rights which are essentially permissive in character. It means, rather, that such principles and conceptions be amplified, amended, and supplemented by others in which the generosity and good will of man's ethical consciousness at its best may be more discriminatingly expressed and extended.

IV

In preparing this essay, I already had a fairly clear idea of what I wanted to say about rights as such. The terms youth, adulthood, and maturity, which have been little studied by analytical philosophers, turned up some surprises: connotations I assumed to be straightforward turned out to have some curious angles, and both affinities and disaffinities I had taken for granted faded on closer scrutiny. As a preliminary exercise I have as usual consulted the *Oxford English Dictionary,* a book which, if not always profound, is useful when one wants to see in outline the lay of a conceptual land.

Youth, we are told, has three main connotations, some of them more perplexing than they may seem at first glance: (a) the fact or state of being young and, more figuratively, newness and recentness; (b) that phase of life between childhood and adult age, and again more figuratively, any early stage of existence and (c) the qualities characteristic of the young, for example, freshness, vigor, vitality, creativity and (more pejoratively) wantonness and rashness. What shall we say of all this? To take the last point first, it should be noted that although many youths do appear rash or wanton in the eyes

of their elders, and some of them doubtless are so by any
standards, rashness is endemic to the human species, and that
every stage of life presents its own forms of liability in this
regard. The much discussed movie, *The Graduate,* whatever
may be said of its artistic merits, certainly suggests that
middle age is a time of immense hazards in both directions
especially among the affluent. It also raises the question
whether some of the rashness and most of the wantonness
ascribed to youth may be functions of the examples set for
it by people in the life-stage ahead. More interesting, however, is the likelihood that those forms of rashness and wantonness to which youths as such may be prone are merely deviant
expressions of their other, more positive powers of freshness,
vitality, vigor, imaginativeness, and creativity. In any case, what
the potentially rash and wanton of all ages need are not so
much laws that restrict their liberties as knowledge to inform
their vigor and vitality, and better opportunities for significant
love and affection. More positive freedoms, not fewer negative
ones, are the primary cures for these faults where they exist.

The second connotation, which distinguishes youth as that
phase of life between childhood and adult age, raises many
questions. Plainly it does not refer merely to a specific term
of years. Many people retain the qualities and powers, as
well perhaps as the vulnerabilities mentioned above, until
well beyond their middle twenties; and some precocious youngsters
enter upon the age of youth before their teens, just as others
remain children, in effect, all their lives. Clearly the age of
youth turns less upon questions of time than upon qualities
of being, and in the following discussion I shall so treat it.

More puzzling are the relationships between youth and
adulthood. If, for example, one understands by an adult one who
is mature in a purely biological sense, then obviously many youths
are as adult as they will ever be, and a great many fortunate
adults are still youths. Evidently biological factors cannot be
decisive here. On the other hand, if by an adult one refers to
a person who is entitled not only potentially but actually to
enjoy legal or other rights, then, from the perspectives we have
now reached, some youth are fully adult and others not—and vice
versa.

Evidently it is time to take a closer look at the notion of an
adult itself. The central entry in the *Oxford English Dictionary*
tells us that a person is adult when he is "fully developed in mind
and body" or else possessed of full powers of "thought, deliberation, and judgment." On the one side, an adult is a person who
is mature in a certain respect. On the other, he is one who

possesses certain psychological qualifications. Let us leave the notion of maturity aside for the moment. Certainly the powers of thought, deliberation, and judgment, as understood here, are not empirical concepts in the sense of the term currently employed in the so-called behavioral sciences. For while they do indeed have to do with questions of behavior, these are questions of intention and conduct not of mere bodily movements or changes. And it is for just this reason that contemporary behavioral psychology which attempts to correlate forms of bodily "inputs" and "outputs" (as the jargon goes) avoids like the plague all such intentional verbs as "deliberate" and "judge." Unfortunately those concerned with problems about rights of youth cannot settle for input-output correlations, but must deal with psychological concepts of a wholly different sort. What are these?

We many get some leverage by observing that definitions of an adult make reference to a *person* who is developed in certain powers of mind (as well as body). The concept of a person presents many problems. Still, enough is known about its use to make it clear that powers ascribed to persons are not the same sort of thing as the dispositions imputed to mere things or objects of a certain sort. Now as its etymological root *(persona)* suggests, the concept of a person is normally employed in speaking of someone or something to whom (or which) certain desirable roles or functions are ascribed.[1] Accordingly, a person is one who is assigned particular offices and duties, prerogatives and rights, and the psychological powers imputed to him are those required in order to perform the roles and fulfill the functions in question. Hence in speaking of an adult as a person who is fully developed in mind (and body) we are at the very least ascribing to him mental powers, not pertaining to individuals of a certain age, but necessary to certain forms of achievement, in virtue of which he is entitled to perform relevant actions and, in some circumstances, may be held liable if he fails to perform them.

Adulthood is therefore not just any sort of maturity, and so far as youths and their rights are concerned this is a matter of great importance. Thus, while we may speak of mature lions, elm trees, or parsnips, we would not, I believe, ever regard them as adults. The mature lion must meet certain specifications, but they do not suffice to make him adult because they give him no status as a person. What is required of adults, unlike merely mature creatures of a certain breed or species, are mental powers

1. This point becomes obvious enough when we recall what is involved, for example, in the concepts of legal, moral, or religious persons.

pertaining to the fulfillment of roles pertinent or perhaps indispensable to the aims of some institution, society, or way of
life. And in such matters, questions of age in particular seem
entirely secondary.

V

Are questions of age secondary in these matters? Up to this
point I can well imagine that both young and old readers may
feel, from their respective stations, that hitherto my remarks
about the concepts of youth have been too abstractly functional-
istic. What has been left out are the sheer unalterable facts
of age and aging. The first entry on youth in *Oxford English
Dictionary* reminds us that youth is the fact or state of being
young. Thus, while Leonard Bernstein still may be the most
youthful of middle-aged Americans, he is no longer a youth,
whereas the teen-age supporters of Senator Eugene McCarthy
are youths, whatever the quality of their political wisdom or
moral rectitude. From the standpoint of the older generation,
it may be argued further that although conceptions of adulthood are indeed tied to social practices or attitudes, there
remain basic universal functions of adults in all historical
societies, to which the thoroughly exoteric powers of judgment,
deliberation, and thought have always been indispensable. In
short, adults are and must be people of mature age who must
share the primary responsibilities of ordinary social life: the
responsibilities of earning a living, parenthood, citizenship,
performing the tasks essential to keeping of the basic institutions of society in working order. Thus older people, by and
large, have and must continue to set the standards of adulthood,
for their judgment, however fallible, is what we finally must
rely upon. This sounds very concrete. Unhappily (or happily,
depending upon one's attitudes) other things are also concrete.
I can imagine many intelligent, well-educated, and dedicated
young people replying as follows: if youth connotes not only
the fact or state of being young but, more figuratively, also
newness and recentness one thing is clear: we do indeed live
in a society whose institutions are not only run by old people,
but which is itself old, and like most old things arthritic, incapable of making the freshly-conceived decisions and adjustments
essential to the survival of the very society and its institutions
which our putative adults cherish. For example, in our system it
is next to impossible for any but dodos to be elected President
of the United States, and much the same holds with respect to
the major managerial jobs of the great corporations, the great
universities and foundations, and the military and police forces.

Even our dictionaries are compiled by conventional scholars who
reflect both the habits of speech and the attitudes of our *de facto*
adults whose powers of judgment and thought are all too well
suited to the "business" of a society which is no longer a
light to the world. In most important situations, our young
people are indeed treated not as adults but as persons occupying
ambiguous positions between childhood and adult age. In
practice they are at best merely pre- or potential adults who
may one day become adults *if* they behave themselves and
submit to the forms of judgment and thought of those who
effectively control the policies and activities of our major
institutions. But what about those who resist or radically dissent,
those who "opt out"? Will they be allowed to become adults?
Business is indeed business, and the more unconventional the
youth the more systematically he is excluded from its decisive
transactions and operations.

Let us, however, as friends of youth insist, like the greying
eminences themselves, that all concrete realitites be taken into
account. Speaking as presumptive youths therefore, we will accept,
subject only to qualifications that "our" experience shows to be
realistic, the conditions of adulthood that existing adults regard
as *sine qua non:* judgment, deliberation, and thought. In pass-
ing we may observe that most existing institutions—political,
legal, education, and religious—are systematically calculated to
delay our acquisition of the powers of judgment necessary to
established ways of adult life. And if from our elders' point
of view we are too often rash and wanton, is not the fault theirs
as much as ours? Or rather is it not owing to a prevailing
social order that compels us, even from our own point of view,
to take long shots, to take our fun where we can find it and to
make up our own games as we go along? However, speaking
soberly and concretely, we already possess powers that entitle
us to the sort of adulthood which a decent contemporary
society would accept as a matter of course. Take the matter
of thought, essential to sensible deliberations and judgments
in affairs of government. We know more about the world, human
and otherwise, possess more finely honed conceptual and intellectual skills than all but a handful of our elders. However, let
us not only concede, but insist that knowledge of matters of
fact is not the only thing essential to sound deliberations and
judgments. What is wanted also is the capacity for emotional
development, powers of imagination, sympathy and affection, the
capacity for idealism and of identification with great causes,
such as those inscribed, for example, in our own *Declaration
of Independence* and our *Bill of Rights*. These surely should

be the auxiliary powers of adult persons capable of making the great decisions upon which not only our well-being but our very lives depend.

Yet (speaking once more in my own person) if the freshest, most imaginative of our contemporary psychologists are to be believed, it is in the age of youth that men possess these powers more abundantly than at any other time of life. Surely our own experience during this troubled and immensely troubling period in our history confirms this. I am not forgetting the contributions of some young people to the disorders that made repression the great theme of both political parties in the 1968 presidential campaign. But surely if adult Americans have learned anything from history it is that repression—call it "law and order" if you prefer—is the last response which creative minds should make to the general disorders to which our youths have contributed their own destructive bit. Repression is the response not of wise adults but of men who have lost the powers of reflection that can enliven the judgments, political and otherwise, our people so desperately need. Our great trouble is not lawlessness but something far worse: the loss among our law-abiding leaders of what Matthew Arnold called that saving "sweetness" of spirit, which, in calling men to order, conveys at the same time a sense not of hardness but of care, not of a desire to hang on to one's own but to share it, not of a demand for "justice," which here becomes another word for retribution, but of need for rehabilitation and reunion. But what is true of our leaders is true of ourselves who have chosen or permitted them to represent us. In the end the only response to anarchy, as Arnold knew, must be from that cultivation and elevation of the spirit which adds the sweetness of the heart to the light of the mind. And we "adults" seem incapable of making that response in any sustained and moving way worthy of emulation among our own offspring.

I am not unaware that, so far as our contemporary youth are concerned, Matthew Arnold can hardly be regarded as our man in the 19th century. That is partly why I have mentioned him rather than, say, Nietzsche or Kierkegaard. But he is also worth remembering here, not only because he himself tried in his own unflinching Victorian way to find a way toward understanding and meeting the responsibilities of adulthood in a time which was after all a prelude to our own, but because he himself, as he knew, all too well was afflicted in his own phrase with "this strange disease of modern life," an illness from which another writer, closer in style to ourselves, William James, also suffered throughout his life. What is the disease?

It has many names, but scepticism will do.

What does scepticism mean in the sphere that here concerns us: the sphere of judgment and deliberation and hence not of purely theoretical but also of practical reason whose aim is choice and action? Here, where James like Arnold knew whereof he spoke, scepticism means on the one side loss of faith, of concern for loyalty and trust, and on the other a failure of will. Judgment is listless, spectatorial, and therefore pointless unless it moves the will. And it is sporadic, desperate, merely compulsive, unless it is infused with faith and the vital urgency which is the offspring of faith. Yet if Erikson is even half right, it is in the age of youth that these qualities of being still exist as actualities, not as something to be recovered for a dying moment through someone else's rhetoric. As every teacher knows, he needs his students more than they need him. For they enable him first of all to perceive that *his* scepticism is not the result of uncynical wariness and experience but all too often of a disabling, self-protective, loss of heart. It is our students and our children who bring us back to life by showing us the preciousness and precariousness of all significant human beings, without which ordinary adulthood, with all its pretense of "judgment" and "deliberation," and indeed the whole business of practical reason becomes a dreary farce which we run through each day for want of something better to do. It is youth, by forcing us to reconsider our "principles" (which for the most part are merely the routine responses of party men, professional men, members of a social class), that helps us to recover a significant, functional scepticism out of which could emerge a new idea or a fresh hope for our kind,

How little do we know ourselves, we adult Americans, managers of the world's greatest novelty shop? What do we sell there that could make us new men? We are masters of gadgetry. But we have let our institutions, once examples to all mankind, become rigid and lethargic, unresponsive to serious demands for rapid social change. In our fear of the outside world we outdo the Russians themselves. Who are our statesmen and preceptors? They are, quite literally, creations of cosmeticians, ghost writers, image-makers, and pollsters. Thought, deliberation, judgment: what an incredibly sad joke it is that at the circuses where major parties pretend to conduct the deliberations that are supposed to enable a great democracy to make reasonable judgments, by whom and how it shall be ruled, these balding eagles can find no visible way of demonstrating their manhood except to surround themselves with flag-waving children, pin-up girls, rosy-cheeked daughters and handsome sons, and (slightly less obvious) cadres of sleek, well-groomed young bodyguards. Youth: only its circumambient image seems able to prove, either to themselves or to their audiences, that they even exist. But all they want is the image; the presence, the actuality of youth is too frightening. Real youths, serious youths who have proven their adulthood, are held at bay by mace, tear gas, and night sticks. How can this tragedy be stopped? How can a democratic people renew its strength? Only, I am convinced, by enabling all youths to participate fully in forming the judgments of our common social and institutional life. Only, that is to say, by enabling them to view themselves as adults. If some of them are not yet mature—as I realize—then we ourselves can match them two for one. But, young or old, one learns to walk by walking and until our youth walks, our society will remain in a wheel chair.

VI

Thus, by pondering the meanings and applications of the terms of our discourse in some of the concrete circumstances of their contemporary use we are brought directly around to the immense problem of this essay: rights of youth. Notice, however, that I have spoken only of "rights" not of "the rights" of youth. For I am concerned in the first instance with moral rights, and only in consequence with the political, legal, educational, and other institutional rights which reflective men may consider to be ascribable to youths in the modern age. We have seen that rights do not exist apart from responsibilities, and that the sense of moral responsibility, as exponents of the new morals have taught us, must begin at home where free and sober men can discover their own moral commitments. Therefore, I propose to begin by asking in the form of an imaginative experiment, not what rights young people may claim of some abstract entity called "mankind," but what sorts of rights enlightened young people may ascribe to and claim of one another, when viewed as members of a distinct moral community.

Let us suppose them to be reflective, tolerably informed, and generously inclined yet disposed also to give a certain primacy to the claims of their own community: call it, for convenience, "the league of youth." This sense of priority, as they themselves recognize, stems partly from a sense of exclusion and hence of alienation from the prevailing institutional and social life of the American system. More positively it stems also from a

sense of their identity with one another as youths, as well
as from an awareness both of stress and of opportunity which
distinguish them not merely from their elders but in some
measure from previous generations of young people. Owing to
the existence of the various media and forms of transportation
which make possible virtually immediate communication with
other youths, both at home and abroad, they realize that
community for them (as well as for others) is no longer a
function of geographical closeness, of superficial cultural
similarities, of ties owing to accidents of birth and nurture
in a particular town or country or social class. For this and
other reasons, they feel themselves to be the bearers of a new
culture which, if allowed to spread, could assist in the rejuvena-
tion of the whole race of men. Perhaps it is not too fanciful to
say that they view themselves as filling an historic role in our
time somewhat analogous to the roles which other reformist and
revolutionary classes believed they played during the great
revolutionary ages between the 18th and early 20th centuries
in America and Europe. And if this imposes upon them special
responsibilities it also disposes them to regard one another
as possessing certain correlative rights. Analogously they feel a
kinship with contemporary revolutionary movements in Latin
America, in Africa, and in Asia, and they consider all dis-
franchised and disadvantaged people as having transnational
and trans-cultural rights which they, as members of the league
of youth, should defend as advocates.

Some have called them "anarchists" because they talk of
"participatory democracy," because they engage in seemingly
unorganized, isolated, and gratuitous acts "against the system."
This, I think, is a shallow view. Although militant, they abhor
all military and para-military forms of organization and unity.
Actually they are trying out forms of organization, inspired
in part by men like Gandhi, that require both extraordinary
self-lessness and self-discipline. Perhaps they will fail in this,
but what a pity if they do. For, if I understand them, their view
is that the alternative is not gradual piecemeal progress through
"legitimate" institutional channels, but very conceivably a dead
planet. And more generally, in a time of unique danger not for
themselves alone but for *their* successors—their children and their
students—it is not their task only but a right which they bestow
upon one another to serve as agents of a general spiritual and
social reformation. And it is in terms of this right that they
justify their continuing resistance to "the system" and their
exemplary acts of extreme refusal and defiance. What appear
from a conventional moral or legal point of view to be acts of

immorality or rebellion are consequences of collateral obligations which their rights as active members of the league of youth entail.

Some foolish spokesmen for the league of youth profess to be contemptuous of the liberal tradition. Yet in many ways our youths strike me as reaffirming a fundamental contention of that tradition, which views rights primarily as permissions or liberties to do as one pleases without interference, particularly in the sphere of personal life. In fact, I should argue that one of the salient characteristics of their community is their insistence on extending the range of such permissions, in matters not only of taste, including such things as dress, manners, and modes of speech, but also more importantly of sex. However, they do not equate personal freedom with privacy. And whereas the Victorian liberals and their Bloomsbury successors were often very free indeed in sexual as well as in other matters of personal life, they performed their rites behind closed doors in thick-walled houses well back from the road. Here I think we must see that in the classical liberal tradition there was a deep connection between the rights or permissions, associated with personal liberty and the rights pertaining to private property. I have a right to do as I please in my house or in houses where I am invited, in such affairs as sex because this is the proper sphere of personal life. I have no such right—just the contrary—in public places where, presumably, my roles are no longer purely or primarily personal. On this score the league of youth, less concerned with private property and possessions, are at once more permissive about what may be done in public and less observant of rights of privacy. What shouldn't be done in public simply shouldn't be done at all, and what is permissible in private is in effect permissible anywhere. In this respect their sense of community, like that of the Socialists, is so strong that they can scarcely understand why anyone should claim rights to privacy, where in the name of liberty the individual for the time being cuts himself off from his kind.

This of course creates an impression of vulgarity, of callousness, of plain indecency among solid citizens who in their carefully guarded penthouses and suburban homes feel free to do just as they please, however debased or debasing. I have no doubt that there is here a profound generation gap, but it is closely tied to different primary attitudes, regarding both the sense of community and something entirely different: the institutions belonging to a social system. Accordingly, that generation gap is accompanied by radical differences in regard to the moral claims which people may lay upon one another in the names both of negative and of positive freedom. Solid citizens, quite properly from their point of view, begin their deliberations concerning their own moral responsibilities toward other members of society by reflecting upon their various institutional rights which they assume at the same time to have a *prima facie* moral claim upon themselves and others. The members of the league of youth, enjoying only a modicum of such rights, and thinking of themselves in the first instance as members of a community which the society does not even realize to exist, attach no such moral significance to the institutional rights in question. Therefore, what are virtually indefeasible rights to their elders are for them functions of social policies whose worth appears to them entirely problematic.

The implication is plain: if youths are to think as solid citizens, attaching an inherent moral significance to the institutional rights of the social system, they must be transformed into solid citizens. This can only be done by treating them as full-fledged adult members of the system who can therefore make some identification with its institutions. They must possess these rights, moreover, not merely potentially, but also actually and in full.

Now we have to consider briefly another dimension of the moral outlook of the league of youth which is profoundly at variance with a deep stratum in our cultural tradition and which has been reinforced in recent years by the advent of the graduate university and the commanding position of the university among the primary institutions of our emerging national society. For want of a better term, I shall call this aspect of our tradition "rationalism," and indeed it does derive, as an ideology, largely from the writings of the great classical philosophers beginning with Plato and Aristotle. From this point of view, human normality and maturity are derived from a conception of man as "the rational animal" whose highest good is knowledge, and whose highest knowledge is of the sort we nowadays call "scientific." Further, possession of the intellectual powers and skills necessary to the achievement of such knowledge is itself an evidence of wisdom and hence of a *prima facie* right to leadership, if not to rule, within the society. A democratic society like our own professes to deny this intellectual elite the right to rule, but increasingly it bestows upon it an informal but nonetheless powerful right to be heard, to advisory positions of immense prestige and power, and of course to leadership and governance within the university itself. Let me quote a recent candid formulation of this point of view by Professor George Kateb in an essay, "Utopia and the Good Life." In his defense of the life of the mind, Kateb acknowledges the importance of "educated feelings" and the significance of play in that life. He speaks of the values of "playing at life," and of its virtue in the "enrichment of character" and in enabling people to "experience the higher pleasures" which, however, must be kept under control by the higher faculties. What are these faculties? Kateb's answer is revealing:

> . . . play is play: there must be some steadiness, some seriousness in the midst of this release and fluidity. Once again, the cultivation of higher faculties provides the answer. Greater in seriousness than even the making of beautiful objects and the doing of glorious deeds is the life of knowing. . . . We would compound the intellectualist heresy and say that man possessed of the higher faculties in their perfection is the model for utopia and already exists outside it. . . .[2]

Kateb, a very up-to-date Plato, makes it clear that no "metaphysical theory" of the world underlies this contention. He is talking as plain scholar in behalf of the plain, factual knowledge to which the contemporary university *professor and researcher aspires,* which decidedly does *not* include such *outré* matters as, the knowledge of God, the playful knowledge of the lover of Mozart, or the presumptive wisdom of sages and prophets.

It must suffice to say that Mr. Kateb, no doubt happily, does not belong to what I have called the league of youth. For one thing they conceive the life of the mind in very different terms from the tradition which he represents. They do not despise scholarship certainly, but they are more skeptical of the undisputedly supreme worth of investigations of which the sciences provide a paradigm, and of the tendency, from the Greek philosophers onward, to view the arts either as inferior vehicles of knowledge or else as expressions of emotion and feeling which are therefore of secondary value. The new youth tends to view man's higher faculties and indeed the whole life of the mind itself in less abstractly intellectualistic and hierarchical terms. Accordingly they regard the prerogatives of science in the educational sphere and the rights of scientifically oriented youths as in no sense primary or preemptive. The love of truth, particularly as the scholar-scientist views it, is only one of the major passions of the mind. In a certain way, the deep vein of equalitarianism which is elsewhere such a persistent

2. Cf. "Utopia and the Good Life," from *Utopias and Utopian Thought,* edited by Frank E. Manuel. The Daedalus Library, published by Houghton Mifflin Company and the American Academy of Arts and Sciences, 1966, p. 257.

theme among members of the new youth also shows itself here in the equal respect it pays scientists, poets, painters, dancers, and philosophers.

Beyond this, however, they find distasteful the whole mentality which so delights in ranking "glorious deeds" below (or above) other forms of action. Imaginative works of love and affection are as wonderful and often as difficult as any others. Why should we not accept them with the same regard as we accord other manifestations of human genius? But this brings us finally to corresponding differences between their religious attitudes and those of many exponents of the Judeo-Christian tradition for whom the supreme, not to say the only authentic religious act, is comprehended exclusively in such phrases as "the love of God." Most of them are unorthodox. But I am impressed both by their sustained religious seriousness and by their tolerance for all genuine expressions of the sense of the holy and the wonderful. In fact, among no group in our time is the sense of the *profane* in our common social life a source of greater sorrow. Indeed, it is the absence of any authentic religious spirit in the routines of conventional institutional activity which makes them despair of their human worth.

VII

In bringing this discussion of youth and its rights toward a conclusion, I now propose to shift perspectives, moving outside the league of youth to a conceivably wider community of human beings of which the members of that league may well (and as I think rightly) regard themselves as members. In the first instance, however, I shall continue the discussion in essentially ethical terms. It is for this reason that I have stressed the term "community" here rather than "society" or "social system." As here understood a community is not itself an institution or network of institutions, though it may establish institutions that serve in various ways as its agencies.[3] An individual can be the member of a society against his will; he may also in some measure fulfill the functions of a class or perform the functions assigned to him by a social system while feeling little or no sense of moral obligation in doing so. Or like many of us, he may be self-divided in this respect, proceeding by stages from dissent to resistance, and from thence to rebellion and revolution according to the quality and direction of that self-division. But one cannot revolt against

3. By an institution here I have in mind such things as banks, courts of laws, electoral colleges, and universities.

a community; one can only leave it, cease to acknowledge oneself as one of its members. This is because a community is by definition like a "congregation" of religious worshippers: it has no reality or meaning save insofar as its members conceive of themselves as belonging to one another in continuing relations of mutual trust and respect. In short, one cannot be the member of a community without feeling a basic moral responsibility to it and to its members.

While it is impossible to conceive of anyone as being the member of a community, in the sense I have in mind, without enjoying certain rights, which are among the conditions of membership, there seems to me no logical reason to suppose that every member of a community should have exactly the same rights and responsibilities. Accordingly, I shall make a distinction between two sorts of communal rights, one generic, the other more special. Although as one may well imagine, every member of a community might properly claim a right to life and to as much negative freedom as is compatible with the survival and the pursuance of other primary ends of the community, it might also be agreed that certain rights are to be enjoyed or enjoyed in full only by certain members of classes thereof. For example, elderly persons no longer capable of fending for themselves might properly claim rights to certain forms of protection or to comforts to which other members of a community have no rightful claim.

Now let me emphatically assert that if youths are to be regarded as members of the wider community of men of which I have spoken, their youth does not exempt them from responsibilities pertaining to the generic rights of all of its members. Thus they must (let us assume) respect or even be obliged to protect, in many situations, the lives of their fellows, and they must at the same time respect the negative freedoms of other members.[4] However, in this essay our concern is primarily with rights of youth, and it is their special rights within the community of men that now concern me, and in particular those rights that derive not from their common powers of judgment and deliberation, nor even from their capacities to acquire or develop such powers—their potentialities that is as "adults"—but rather from the qualities of their youth itself. Here our earlier psychological and conceptual analyses provide indispensable clues. Specifically, I have in mind

4. Here as elsewhere we may also reasonably assume that rights like responsibilities are rarely, if ever, absolutely unconditional; they hold as we say, *ceterus paribus,* so that it may on occasion be necessary to perform acts that radically limit or override a particular right.

among the special rights of youth in the wider community of
men those necessary for them to fulfill themselves as youths:
their enormous capacities for learning, invention, and creation.
But also quite unsentimentally I believe it all the more necessary
to stress in these days, when pundits talk endlessly of "law and
order," their extraordinary problems of love and companionship,
identity and self-discovery, in virtue of which they should
have rights to a special tolerance, patience, and quiet assis-
tance that are more extensive than older members of the wider
community may decently claim for themselves. And if this tolerance and patience are not forthcoming, and they are not accordingly protected against the thuggery of police and the retributive
justice of benighted administrators of the draft, the price in
alienation and dissociation from the wider community will be
a calamity not for themselves alone but for us all.

But the preceding sentence places the accent in the wrong
place. For the proper emphasis here should be on the positive
endowment of young people, not potentialities from which other
presumably more mature powers may come if they are to be
accorded liberties "we" would not claim for ourselves. This
endowment, in the age of youth, is already at flood tide, in
some respects as strong and mature as it will ever be. Save for
unconscionable accident, a Keats or a Schubert, a Pascal or a
Frank Ramsey might have gone on in later years to fulfill a genius
at which the rest of us could only marvel. This is no way
blunts my point. At eighteen or twenty or twenty-five many
men are more "mature" than they will ever be again and have
already done things—performed "glorious deeds," created
"beautiful objects," discovered theorems—which are as splendid,
as lovely, as true as the human spirit and mind can ever achieve.

From this I conclude that in certain directions rights of
youth are not in the least like the rights of "minors": the
rights, that is, of potential adults or the potential rights of
adults. They are rights in full being that belong to youth itself,
and if these rights carry with them subsidiary rights to forgive-
ness and excuse, this only proves the greatness and the wisdom—
the adulthood—of the great community of men which I have in
mind and to which I aspire to belong. This is not to suggest
that every youth is a genius, or every young person just because
he is young is a great benefactor of the human race. It is to
say rather that there exist dimensions and possibilities of
experience as fully realized in youth as they are likely ever to
be again, and hence that the great community of men owes them
special consideration in the form of rights of youth which by
the nature of the case can involve no corresponding obligations

on the part of youths to other members of that community. I have argued that generically rights are not practices, but now I can use the point more forcefully by saying that such rights ought, as far as possible, to be translated into social practices in the form both of economic supports and of continuing educational aid, fellowships, grants in aid, and the life which will afford them the leisure necessary to fulfill themselves as youths. Too often in our society youth is treated either as a period of rapid preparation for adult life or else as a time in which, if they have no special intellectual or artistic talents, youths should be put to work at jobs that are menial, less interesting, and less rewarding than those of their elders. Older people we sometimes think have thereby earned the right to an increasingly early retirement, a time of leisure, in which to do as they please. But an affluent society, were it wise, should extend wherever possible to the young comparable periods or intervals of prolonged leisure in which they too could follow their bent as youths. In short, an inconceivably wealthy society like ours might well turn its immense economic and technological resources to the liberation of all young people from the full necessities comprehended under the phrase "earning a living." One can even look forward to an age in which it will be time enough to start earning a living after one has lost the bloom of youth. Nor is there any need to view such a period of leisure as a period either of idleness or of more extended preparation for the rigors of later life. Just the contrary. It is possible, moreover, to envisage forms of education, artistic, intellectual or cultural activity in which, instead of being taught by elders who seek to pass on skills, forms of knowledge, technical or otherwise, which they as elders greatly prize, young people would do better to teach one another in ways that are appropriate to their own perspectives and interests and that develop powers which youths as such find worthy of cultivation. Institutions of higher learning of and not merely for the young need not be separated entirely from existing institutions, and multiversities which contain schools of dentistry and departments of home economics, not to mention the burgeoning cross-departmental area studies that enlist the energies of teachers trained in widely different disciplines, might very well establish "colleges" in which, at the same time, the young could engage in forms of study whose content, modes of instruction, and personnel they themselves largely determine.

Finally a word must be said about those more generic human rights which, at present, youths possess to a large degree only in potency. The odd thing about the present situation is that although we like to pretend that owing to their immaturity they are also exempt from many of the responsibilities of adult persons, many harsh and dangerous responsibilities are now borne mainly by young people that require of them skills, understanding, and judgment at least as complex as those possessed by their elders. Further, when we consider the subtle problems of conscience which must be confronted, for example by youthful dissenters and conscientious objectors, it is evident that we expect of them forms of moral development and powers of religious and ethical discrimination at least as advanced as those which older persons fancy they possess. However, the age of youth especially in our time has proved itself to be an age of moral idealism and dedication which fully entitles our youths to enjoy in act most or all of the generic rights we claim for ourselves. As I have elsewhere remarked, a young person mature enough to understand what it may mean to die for his country is also old enough to decide or to help to decide whether the cause is worth dying for.

It is a fact that despite various breakdowns in our school systems, including our institutions of higher learning, many young people in virtue of their extraordinarily extensive informal as well as formal educations are vastly more developed as persons than either the youths of twenty or thirty years ago, when I myself was young, or the middle-agers the youths of that time have now become. Like many of my academic colleagues, I find to my acute embarrassment that many of my students are not only more sensitive and imaginative than I am—that I take for granted—they are also more cultivated and in some respects by my own standards wiser. For, among other things, they know in the fullest sense how near to death is all mankind. I am astonished both by the gentleness of their manners and by the simplicity of their lives. And if drugs are a problem for them, they or their analogues are problems for us all. It goes without remark that in the face of all the forms of suffering, mental as well as physical, with which our society and its institutions have threatened them or else inflicted upon them over and over again, their courage shames us all. Neither dismissal from college, social harassment and ostracism, jail, injury, or murder deflect them from their determination to see not only that justice is done themselves, but also that our whole society commit itself to that reawakening of the community of spirit which begins with justice but ends with great-heartedness and love. By any standards that we, their elders, may in reason apply to ourselves, they have attained adulthood.

This being true, the problem of their political and legal rights in principle pretty well takes care of itself. The state and the legal system, so far as they strive to be just and to serve the common good, deserve respect from members of the party of humanity. However, the state and the legal systems are not ends in themselves, but serviceable agencies of human communities. Or if they may sometimes be more, it is so only insofar as they become primary carriers and symbols of man's communal life. Hence no political and legal order that deserves our loyalty can be repressive or deny to any member of the human community which it serves and symbolizes any right relevant to the maintenance and progress of that order. There can be no quarrel with the thesis that the state, as an agency of that community, may properly be viewed as a guardian that in effect holds in trust the rights of children, of the senile, or the insane. But despite Plato, it cannot be a guardian to adult citizens. Thus if as I claim, our youth is adult and already belongs to the human community in the most active sense of the term, then it is entitled to every legal and political right required for participation in the political process.

Such rights we must remember cannot include merely negative liberties, permissions to vote, run for office, and the rest. For important as they may be, they do not remotely suffice for effective citizenship. Hence such negative liberties must be implemented by rights that enable their full and proper exercise. In the case of youth, particularly, this means above all more and better education. For in the modern age education is virtually the condition of all the other positive freedoms, economic and political, as well as intellectual and spiritual. But education decidedly is not enough, even if our educational system were, as it so tragically is not, up to its own responsibilities. Youths must therefore be entitled to all the forms of social security, as we call it, required for realization of their powers not simply as youths but as citizens.

These, I have been told, are utopian dreams. Are they? If so, responsibilities begin in dreams, and unless someone holds himself responsible, as we have seen, rights do not exist. With all possible emphasis I say it: they had better not remain dreams forever. For youth is not only restless; it is also knowledgeable and determined. As never before it has reached an understanding of its own identity, its strength, its indispensability to any advanced social system like our own. But this is no reason to be afraid. Rather is it a reason for us, not their guardians but their advocates and friends, to make certain that the league of youth remains part of the good society of which the word "America" was once a symbol. For only we ourselves can finally drive them out.

6

The Teaching of
Moral Beliefs

BERTRAM BANDMAN

Hamlet: Denmark is a prison.
Rosencrantz: We think not so, my lord.
Hamlet: Why then, tis none to you; for there is nothing either good
or bad but thinking makes it so; to me it is a prison.

William Shakepeare
From *Hamlet*

Will: But if the cause be not good, the king . . . hath a heavy reck-
oning to make . . . It will be a black matter for the king that
led them to it.

William Shakespeare
From *King Henry V*

WE speak of the moral beliefs we hold and teach to the young
as when affirming the pledge of allegiance: "I pledge allegiance
to the flag of the United States of America and to the Republic
for which it stands, one nation, under God, indivisible, with
liberty and justice for all." Not all our beliefs are of the pledge
variety, however. Such beliefs as the way to bring up children
are held and taught in the hope that the young grow up to
accept them.

We try to teach the difference between right and wrong in
the elementary and secondary level. We make the effort because
we feel that we are charged with this responsibility. Teaching
right from wrong figures among the pre-occupations of pedagogues,
teachers, philosophers, judges, and parents. The charge has
been to establish a worthy and justifiable basis for teaching
children which moral beliefs to accept or reject.

Emotivists hold that moral beliefs like the pledge may have
emotive meaning but lack cognitive meaning. They say such
beliefs are neither true nor false. Others, following the example
of J. L. Austin, contend that to pledge is to perform an act,
much like making a marriage vow or christening a boat. In so

doing one can be either sincere or not, but the vow or pledge one makes cannot be true or false.[1]

Others hold that beliefs, like the pledge of allegiance, are not merely emotive or first person avowals labelled "sincere" or "insincere." Our stock of moral beliefs are true or false or in a significant sense right or wrong. Only under the latter assumption can we teach the difference between right and wrong.

The tendency of the times is to celebrate the view that one's thinking makes a thing good or bad, that putting one's heart into it and having consistency tests applied to one's first person avowals distinguishes good from evil.

I reject this abridgement of responsibility and maintain that a cause, act, thing, person, or belief can be either good or bad, and that no amount of thinking to the contrary can change its being so. I shall argue that (1) there is a justifiable difference between right and wrong (due not solely to our thinking), (2) this difference is a necessary condition for our ability to teach moral beliefs, and (3) in the presence of (1) and (2) we can decide which moral beliefs should be taught.[2]

Two Kinds of Beliefs

We might first distinguish two kinds of beliefs. "I believe in my country, right or wrong" can readily be seen to be different from "I believe that the Empire State Building is the tallest building in the world." The first of these kinds we might call "dispositional" (or "attitudinal") and the second we might call "factual." These two kinds of beliefs may also be understood as "believe-in" and "believe-that."[3] It is generally held that "believe-in" statements are not true or false but that "believe-that" statements are true or false. It is more difficult to decide which attitudinal beliefs to teach than to decide which factual beliefs to teach. Should we teach our students to believe in the pledge of allegiance? More generally, what moral beliefs should be taught?

The term "attitudinal belief" refers to what Hare has called a "blik" or habitual way of seeing things. Scheffler calls this "the orientation of the person to the world."[4] The force, if any, of this kind of belief is that it involves whole-hearted commitment

1. J. L. Austin, in fact chides philosophers for being prey to two fettishes, the true/false and the is/ought.

2. Austin maintains that avowals can't be true or false. I shall try to show that avowals like the pledge of allegiance are true or false.

3. R. Abelson, "The Logic of Faith and Belief" in S. Hook, *Religious Experience and Truth*. New York: New York University Press, 1961, pp. 116-129.

4. I. Scheffler, *Conditions of Knowledge*. Fair Lawn, New Jersey: Scott Foresman, 1965, p. 90.

to what one believes. This may help to explain the various social
movements of the day. The value of a belief seen as acceptance of
a way of life, often religiously impelled, is in the development
and outgrowth of what Malcolm calls the "internal point of view."
It presents a way of seeing the world from the inside out as
the result of growing up and learning from the inside rather than
as the result of a conversion from the outside. This enables a
person to put his "whole heart" into what he believes. A belief
construed as an avowal has been thought to be neither a true or
false assertion. Performatives are not true or false. Like marriage
vows, they just are. Beliefs, in this attitudinal sense, are performative.

Other post-Austinians with whom I agree argue that beliefs
can be avowals and can also be true or false. Avowals are not
more trustworthy for being factually unsupportable like a person's
belief in a fortune teller. The difficulty for one who ignores facts
is that he loses the ability to judge fact from fiction. His belief-
in would, if unconnected to factual beliefs, amount to a belief of
horrors, if there ever was one, and fail to provide rational men a
basis for believing in anything. We sometimes say that facts
brought to light may help to change someone's attitude. Psycho-
analysts are apt to call this accompaniment of attitude with fact
(or the blending of these kinds of beliefs) "an orientation to
reality" and its opposite "disorientation."[5] This is a fact which
through Freud's fog-dispelling labor of the earlier part of this
century does skeptics little good to deny. To believe in anything
at all has to mean that somewhere along the line we have to believe that something is the case; or else, to cite one writer, we
would just be "whistling in the dark"[6] and not be able to take
it seriously. Wrench away all factual beliefs on which attitudes
depend for vindication and there is then nothing in which to
believe.

In a similar connection I criticized this position previously
(in my book, *The Place of Reason in Education*): "I confess that
I find it logically odd for a believer to say, 'I am committed to
religious belief X, but I don't care if it's true or false'; for
his faith would come to rest on nothing at all and not differ ap-
preciably from lunacy." Similarly, a person, who pledges his
allegiance but doesn't care if it is true or false seems to believe
in nothing at all.

To believe something is, according to Peirce, James, and

---

5. See K. Horney, *Neurosis and Human Growth*. New York: W. W. Norton, Chapter 3.
6. Bernard Williams "Tertullian's Paradox" in A. Flew and A. MacIntyre, eds. *New Essays in Philosophical Theology*. New York: Macmillan, 1955, p. 210.

Dewey, to make "behavioral commitments."[7] Ryle similarly explains a belief as a tendency to act. To say, "I believe the ice is thin" means I will either not skate or if I do I will skate cautiously.[8] Hampshire goes even further. "A man who with apparent sincerity professed beliefs upon which he never acted . . . would be said to be holding these beliefs in words only, but not truly believing."[9] Philip Smith similarly argues the thesis that a belief implies action.[10] Raziel Abelson takes the Pragmatic interpretation to be inadequate. To say, "I believe the earth is 92 million miles from the sun" is hardly a behavioral commitment except as a linguistic commitment to continue to assert the proposition believed.[11]

In saying "I believe my team will win," I express not so much an action as I do my *approval* or *acceptance,* and this can be enthusiastic or unenthusiastic. Contrary to Hampshire and others, a belief expressed in words is not a belief in words only. It expresses my *approval* or acceptance. To believe is to approve or accept.

According to Abelson, we do not declare our behavioral intentions "without also making a truth claim."[12] Even if a belief implies action, it also implies a truth claim hedged by a qualifying expression that the truth claim is liable to be withdrawn or cancelled if the claim is shown to be false. The difference between "I believe" and "I know" is that "I believe" makes a weaker truth claim than "I know." My belief that my team will win also makes a claim that it will win and this claim will either be verified or falsified. Similarly, my belief that "The earth is 92 million miles from the sun" expresses provisional *acceptance* of that truth claim. This approval or acceptance gives "initial credibility" to the above truth claim. In expressing approval or acceptance, a belief, whether an avowal or pledge, also makes a truth claim. To believe that something is so or to believe in someone is to express approval or acceptance of a claim made. Beliefs make or imply claims.

What is the nature of the claims made or implied by beliefs? Why bother about claims? Whereas we may not always be able

7. R. Abelson, *loc. cit.* p. 120.

8. G. Ryle, *The Concept of Mind.* New York: Barnes and Noble, 1949, pp. 133-135.

9. S. Hampshire, *Thought and Action.* New York: Viking, 1960, P. 159.

10. P. Smith, *Introduction to Philosophy of Education.* New York: Harpers, 1962.

11. R. Abelson, *loc. cit.* p. 121. Israel Scheffler, however, argues that to make a linguistic commitment (of this kind) commits a person to accept a mutually coherent system of sentences which gives "initial credibility" to the statement, "The earth is 92 million miles from the sun." It is the total credibility of the system that gives initial credibility to any sentences within the system. I. Scheffler, "Justification and Commitment" *Journal of Philosophy,* 1954, pp. 180-190.

12. R. Abelson, *loc. cit.* p. 121.

to apply rational strictures to the appraisals of beliefs, particlarly to such difficult moral beliefs as the pledge of allegiance, we may be able to apply rational strictures to the appraisal of the claims made or implied by such beliefs. That is, beliefs may be rationally assessed by noting the nature and kinds of the claims made in the expression of those beliefs. The position advanced here is that a difficulty in the teaching of moral beliefs is the lack of recognition of the role of claims in the expression of moral beliefs; and that distinctions between true and false or right or wrong claims can help us decide which moral beliefs to teach.

THE USE OF BELIEFS TO MAKE CLAIMS

A claim (coming from the Latin word "clamare" meaning to call or shout out) is used either to contend, maintain, or take a stand, to make or express a demand (complaint, charge, suit or *lien*) as in morals or the law, or to make a factual assertion. A claim then may be used (a) to call out or take a stand, (b) to demand that something should be so, or (c) to assert that something is the case or as a combination of two or three of these. As with the word "good," "claim" is a *janus* word; it performs a variety of functions. Black's *Law Dictionary* defines a claim as a "broad comprehensive word" (in Wheeler v. Equitable Life Assurance Society, U.S. 211, Minn., 474, N.W. 2nd ed., 593,596).[13]

A belief makes a claim either that something should be the case, as in a stand or demand, or that something is the case as in an assertion. A belief-in statement takes a stand or makes a demand whereas a belief-that statement makes an assertion.[14] Claims, like beliefs, avowals, pledges, marriage vows, christenings and the rest, are performative. Even in its use as an assertion, a claim is also a demand for recognition, a call to our attention.

The importance of studying claims made or implied by beliefs is the possibility of appraising or checking them. A person can be asked to produce credentials for his claims more directly and frequently than for his beliefs.

Another feature of claims is that we make them. The word "claim" is primarily used as a verb. We make claims. A claim marks out what we do in a speech act. A claim is not to be had or purchased at the corner store.

13. Black's Law Dictionary, 4th Edition, p. 313. The idea of a claim may be even broader than jurists have thought.
14. It should not, however, be construed from this that beliefs are identical with claims. There is overlap in that both believe-that and a claim-that can be construed as assertions. (One could say, however, "I *claim that* you owe me five dollars.") A claim-to usually refers to a demand or interest.

Another characteristic of claims is that they are the exercise of rights but are not themselves rights.[15] Claims are backed by rights. Without rights claims cannot be upheld. The fact that we make claims does not mean that once made claims cannot be denied as well as upheld; they can be and they can also be shown to be true or false or right or wrong. In the law claims are affirmed or denied, for a legal system provides a way to sustain or deny them and hence to check claims made.

THE BACKING OF CLAIMS IN A LEGAL SYSTEM

It has been noted that claims are used (1) to take a stand, (2) to make a demand, or (3) to make a factual assertion. The first use of "claim" is Martin Luther's *Here I Stand*. The stand-taking use of a claim comes closest to its etymological meaning, cla-mare, "to cry out." It is characteristic of some religious existentialists, professional whistlers in the dark, and backyard theosophers as well as misbehaving children.

Two senses of a claim may be distinguished. We may speak of claims, as does William James, as needs, interests, or demands against the world; they "cry out." A recent critic of James, Joel Feinberg, views a claim that cries out against the world, like that of a needy, desperate, fatherless Mexican infant," . . . like an explosion in the desert. . . . . There is no one to hear it."

The *New York Post* recently reported a man who lost several suits against a city in Florida. He slipped and broke his hip and sued the city and lost. After several similar mishaps and court losses in which he was told that these accidents were legally "acts of God," this accident-prone person filed a claim against God. A judge thereupon ruled the case out on the grounds that "the claim was beyond the Court's jurisdiction." The point being illustrated here is that a claim in sense I is a mere crying out, a call to the wild with no one to hear it.[17]

A claim in sense II entails a *jurisdiction,* a court, a system,

15. Some philosophers like G. H. Von Wright identify claims with permissions or rights. Others like Alf Ross identify claims with rightful or upheld claims. See A. Ross, *Directives and Norms*. London: Routledge and Kegan Paul, 1968, pp. 123-128. I disagree with both views. Concerning the first view, a right or permission can back a claim but is not itself a claim. Concerning Ross's view, not all claims are rightful or sustained. Some are denied.

16. J. Feinberg, "Rights, Duties and Claims" in *American Philosophical Quarterly*, Vol. 3, No. 2, 1966, pp. 142-143. One might note his distinction between "claim to" and "claim-that" used in footnote 14 above. I disagree, however, with Feinberg that James is guilty of thinking that a claim is like an explosion in the desert with no one to hear it. James insists on giving concrete backing to obligations which he does by shifting away for *a priori* ideals to the concrete claims of human beings. See W. James, *The Will to Believe*. New York: Dover, 1956, pp. 194-196.

17. See also K. Horney, *loc. cit.* Chapter 2 on "Neurotic Claims." She speaks of a neu-rotic claim as a grossly exaggerated demand upon the world. It is like a crying out with no one to hear it.

a decision-making procedure to adjudicate a claim. A basis for ruling on a claim must be available in order to have a claim heard and considered. We make a claim in sense I whenever a system of credentials that will establish or invalidate it is lacking or when it is not brought before an appropriate court.

A claim in sense I refers to a stand, demand or assertion lacking jurisdiction, backing, credentials or a system of entitlements of any kind, or that is not open to being checked, confirmed or affirmed. Sense II refers to a claim that is open to being judged as either valid or invalid, justified, well-founded or not, provable, with jurisdiction and that can be submitted to an appropriate system, legal or otherwise, for a decision.

A claim in sense II is one that is made within a legal, formal or scientific system of rules. The statements, beliefs, laws and customs are true or false, right or wrong, valid or invalid, well-founded or not, justifiable or unjustifiable *inside* the context of a particular social or legal system.

If a claim is, in addition to being well-founded within a system, also well-founded outside the system as between two systems, then we might speak of it as a claim in sense III. A claim in sense I is without backing or credentials. It is a wild charge. A claim in sense II is proven or provable, well-founded, just, valid, affirmed or warranted within a legal or social system. The preliminary point to be made is that only in sense II or sense III can differences between claims be resolved by appeal to rational procedures or putatively rational procedures. A claim in either of these two latter senses is affirmed or denied by appeal to a system of (supposedly non-arbitrary) rules. The system gives or withholds credibility to the claims made within it. Making a claim, therefore, is not the same as appraising it. One can do the former anywhere merely by shouting, but one can do the latter only by appealing to the rules of a system. Accordingly, the language of the law provides a paradigm, a telling example of the relation between claims and their proof.[18]

A difficulty arises when someone uses a claim in sense I (whether used as a demand or assertion) and then slips after a while into sense II or sense III, and treats his claim as if it were *a priori*.[19] Hospers speaks of *a priori* assumptions as

18. When a claim is made two questions may be asked (1) Has a rule been violated? (2) Did the person against whom a claim is made actually violate a rule without acceptable extenuating circumstances? But whether a claim is finally sustained or defeated, a claimant is not—at least in a court of law—his own judge. Making and sustaining (or denying) claims are distinct operations and both are not performed by the same person for the obvious reason that too often fairness and impartiality would not result.

19. My book (B. Bandman, *The Place of Reason in Education*. Columbus: The Ohio State University Press, 1967), Chapter 1 gives a similar study to the concept of question and answer.

those articles of faith a person refuses to question.[20] True believers are made of such ilk. To slip from a sense I to a sense II claim is capricious. The Purist, however, acknowledges only sense II claims.[21]

Claims cannot be judged, that is, upheld or affirmed, defeated or denied, without a system of rules which confers, grants, or authorizes decisions to be made. For the purpose of deciding between claims a legal system provides a court. Science provides canons of evidence.

There are three provisions that have to be met by court. There first has to be provision for the *recognition of claims.*[22] Recognition of a claim means that a court is willing to hear a case.[23] By giving recognition to a claim, a court declares that a given case falls within the jurisdiction of the court.[24] Recognition involves epistemic considerations. Questions of the nature of evidence and of the physical and perceptual qualities of witnesses are at stake in deciding whether a court has jurisdiction over a given case. Without a way to recognize claims, such as the registration of gold claims or land claims or copyright claims, there would be no way to tell whether a claim was a sense I or a sense II claim, and no way to tell accordingly whether a claim that was *made* was or ought to be *sustained.*

To say "He hit me" to a court presupposes that "hit" is recognized as a legal violation of a right, and that it is not part of a sport, such as boxing, where hitting above the belt is not recognized as an infraction of rules. Rules of recognition are a necessary condition for making claims in sense II. Without such rules there could be no sense attached to the notion of "legal validity" without which, in turn, there could be no legal system and so no basis for ruling on claims that come before a court.[25]

Secondly, there must be rules of adjudication.[26] Without these

20. J. Hospers, *An Introduction to Philosophical Analysis.* Englewood Cliffs, New Jersey: Prentice Hall, Second edition, 1968, p. 187.

21. The purist use of claims is counter to common usage. It precludes one from qualifying claims as being false, denied or poorly founded. As with beliefs, we need to have a way to withdraw, cancel and hedge claims. The Purist's mistake is also the mistake of those who identify claims with rights (Von Wright) or who think we acquire or possess claims (A. Ross). We do not have claims. We make claims, right or wrong and check them or enable them to be checked. In psychiatric terms, Harry Stack Sullivan termed this process "consensual validation."

22. H. L. A. Hart, *The Concept of Law.* Oxford: Clarendon Press, 1963, pp. 92-92, 113.

23. *Words and Phrases,* Vol. 23 A, p. 120. In Wilcons v. Penn Mutual Life Ins. Co. recognition involves "the power to decide rightly or wrongly."

24. C. Bunn, *Jurisdiction in the Courts of the United States,* pp. 11, 58.

25. Rules of recognition also change. The claim to free public education was not recognized at one time. See also Roscoe Pound, "A Survey of Social Interests," *Harvard Law Review,* October, 1943, p. 36.

26. H. L. A. Hart, *loc. cit.* pp. 94-95.

there would be no way to decide cases or to make rulings or judgments between conflicting claims. Adjudications means a court exists to rule on the claims made, either to uphold or to defeat them.[27] The historic case perhaps dates back to King Solomon who must decide between two women, each of whom claims the baby.[28]

Thirdly, there have to be rules for implementing or enforcing claims or applying appropriate sanctions.[29] A claim once upheld by a court means nothing if it is unenforceable. Charles Peirce once remarked that the law is only as good as the power of a sheriff to put his hand on a violator. A legal system without provisions for enforcing the law is the more liable to collapse.

Without all these conditions there would be no point in making a claim. For a judge to say, "I recognize and grant your right to enter your premises but I cannot provide any way for you to exercise that right" is futile. The recognition, adjudication, and enforcement of claims enables rights and powers to be granted and protected, and this is the means by which a legal or political system carries out its commitments to its citizenry.

The study of a legal system shows how criteria for judging the differences between evaluations like "affirm," or "deny," "uphold" or "quash"—and whose moral counterparts are "right" and "wrong"—get their *credibility,*[30] namely from the system. We can accordingly say that while there are claims in sense I, there are no claims in sense II without these three provisions.[31]

The claims we make, moral[32] or otherwise, are like so much shouting in the air without a system with which to judge those

27. Roscoe Pound, *loc. cit.* p. 2.
28. See also Roscoe Pound, "The Theory of Judicial Decision," *Harvard Law Review,* 1923, pp. 648-649 and 947-948 for the role of precedents in judicial decision-making.
29. See Patrick Devlin, *The Enforcement of Morals.* Oxford: The University Press, 1967.
30. I. Scheffler, "Justification and Commitment" *(loc. cit.).*
31. H. L. A. Hart, *loc. cit.* Chapter 10. International Law. Hart points out that the problem of sanctions in international law is not insurmountable since treaty provisions between nations are often kept despite the absence of provisions for enforcing the law (unlike a municipal legal system.
32. For a defense of the idea that the concept of claims applies to morals, that is, that we can speak of moral claims, see Alf Ross, *Directives and Norms, loc. cit.* pp. 136-137. He points out that in the case of promising "the promisee acquires a claim on the promisor for the fulfillment of the promise." The only exception I wish to take with Ross is that a promisee does not acquire a claim. He acquires the right to make a strong (sense III) claim, one with moral backing. It is strong because the promisor has given backing to the promisee's claim for fulfillment of the promise. Thus, a promise implies a right to make a strong claim for the fulfillment of the promise. If the promise is broken it entitles the promisee to make a claim against the promisor. To break a promise violates a moral rule that promises ought to be kept.
Claims imply obligations. A promisee acquires the right to obligate the promisor (under ordinary circumstances) to fulfill the promise.
The main point of this analysis of promises in terms of claims is to support Ross's point that the concept of claims extends to moral language.

claims. Why make claims unless there is a chance to sustain them? Since well-founded claims presuppose a system of some kind, legal or other, the same may be said of moral claims. Without a social system or structure, moral claims are like shoutings in the air. A social system provides criteria for judging moral claims. But as with legal system, there need not be only one moral system or point of view. Indeed, the word "moral," meaning mores or custom, suggests a variety of moral systems or points of view.[33]

What counts as right or wrong depends on a moral system of point of view under which moral claims or demands in sense I are judged. The difference between right and wrong comes not from above or outside but from the *inside* of a system. Judging between moral points of view or between moral system requires a sense III use of the word "claims." (The analogy to international law need not be strained.)

The move from sense II claims (those of a system) to sense III claims (moral claims *writ large*) is more difficult. An example of sense II morality is the Southern morality Mark Twain depicts in *Huckleberry Finn*. Huck's obligation is to turn Jim in, but he doesn't. Huck Finn's act of saving his friend Jim transgresses the mores of his society but it appeals nonetheless to a wider, more humanitarian idea of morality. Students of law term this "publici juris," meaning that prior moral consideration is given to those interests affecting the community at large.[34] We can speak here of higher and lower level moral claims or of claims of wider and smaller generality (corresponding to senses II and III).

There are no claims in sense II or III without standards of appraisal for making claims.[35] Without a court of some kind there is no adjudication, no distinction between a claim and a well-founded claim.[36] Without a comparable moral system in sense III there is no way to judge moral claims as either right or wrong.

How Are Moral Beliefs To Be Judged?

What is the upshot of this study of claims for the teaching of moral beliefs and specifically for deciding whether to teach the pledge of allegiance? Beliefs make or imply claims and the claims

33. See A. MacIntyre, *A Short History of Ethics*. New York: Macmillan, 1966, Chapter 18, pp. 249-269, for an account of alternative moral points of view.

34. For example, preservation of individual and group life seems to be a norm. If, however, overpopulation continues it is conceivable that parents will be urged to eat their young and that this practice will be generally approved.

35. Claims as interests or demands are the sources and limits of our obligations. Outside of them, we owe nothing, cannot be obligated, cannot be told what ought to be the case.

36. Claims are like checks. There can be no checks without a checking account in a banking system.

may sometimes be easier to appraise than beliefs. A legal formal, or factual system provides a basis for affirming or denying a claim. An elucidation of the claims contained in our beliefs may help us decide which beliefs to teach. The remaining portion of this paper is limited to an elucidation of only a portion of one of the above conditions of a legal system, that of adjudication. An effort will be made to show the relevance of adjudication to the teaching of moral beliefs.

We can only tell or teach the difference between right and wrong if we have ample grounds to affirm or deny a moral belief or claim. We previously noted that a legal system provides grounds for judging whether to affirm or deny a claim. One can judge claims within a legal system, in part, because one can deny as well as affirm a claim. By extension of a legal system on only this one point one can tell and so teach the difference between right and wrong if there is also a way to *deny* as well as to affirm a moral belief. For example, if a Christian and a cannibal disagree whether murder is good or bad, I believe they can do so only if each of them can express dissent as well as assent to what the other calls good; otherwise, they could neither argue with nor teach each other that only one of these practices is good. If both practices are mutually praiseworthy, there is no reason for the furor between them. Each is not only commending his own practice, but also condemning the other fellow's practice. Both commendation and condemnation are necessary to a moral dispute because if the dispute is treated so that only one practice is right, it would be self-contradictory to commend both customs. The Christian would not commend gentleness if he did not simultaneously condemn the taking of scalps; nor would the cannibal commend qualities that go with taking large quantities of scalps, unless he too were condemning gentleness. While we commend what we are for, it is also part of every moral decision to condemn what we are against. There would accordingly be no moral discussion or argument in a world where we only used the "good." Moral language gains part of its force by the very real contrast between good and bad. More than being a difference in one's thinking that makes one thing good and another bad, it is a difference between different and opposing states of affairs.

If there is no difference between right and wrong, then when new people invade an island, for instance, the moral language of the new order becomes as easily accepted and as little understood as that of the old order, though what the words signify in terms of their differing moral beliefs is miles apart. Perhaps some such type of moral noneducation contributes to men like Hitler arising and not coming sooner to a bad end.

If there were no other side to a moral argument, the morals of a people would soon be taken not as appraisals or judgments but as descriptions of behavior; and in losing its sense as a term of appraisal, a moral belief would eventually immobilize the ability to oppose what is wrong or to favor what is right.

Dissent, lest it be shortly remembered, no less than assent, has a history of moral doings which is quite indispensable in continually reviving the force and importance of moral appraisal. In this I share Mill's concern with the evil of silencing the expression of an opinion.

. . . the peculiar evil of silencing the expression of an opinion is, that it is robbing the human race . . . posterity as well as the existing generation. If the opinion is right, they are deprived of the opportunity of exchanging error for truth; if wrong, they lose, what is almost as great a benefit, the clearer perception and lovelier impression of truth, produced by its collision with error.[38]

The practical import of the foregoing suggests that as a statement functions as a factual claim or belief if it can be falsified,[39] a statement functions as a moral claim or belief (in sense III) if it can be *denied*. As an assertion has meaning or credibility if one can tell the difference between true and false, so an affirmation or moral belief has meaning or credibility if there is a way to tell the difference between right and wrong. Thus, as a *bona fide* factual belief is falsifiable, a bona fide moral belief is deniable.

The sense of denial intended here does not mean one can or should deny everything willy nilly. It means that one is willing and able to show the grounds for denying one's own affirmation. This means that one's moral beliefs or claims are open to a criticism of their own unsatisfactory implications.[40]

What is morally objectionable about the way moral beliefs are sometimes used with inverted commas is not an affirmation to a way of life but the insistence that it is undeniably right. For the act of striking out the signal for dissent erodes a moral belief into one that is defended by exclusive appeal to extra-moral ordinances. While we may not know what entitles us to speak of having the right moral belief, the extra-moral decree which prohibits dissent

37. Claims are not *sui generis* moral or non-moral. An accident can be factual but have moral consequences. Factual considerations can often help us decide between conflicting claims.

38. J. S. Mill, *On Liberty,* Chapter 2, "Utilitarianism, Liberty and Representative Government." Everyman's Library, p. 79.

39. See K. Popper, "Philosophy of Science: A Personal Report." *British Philosophy in Mid-Century,* C. A: Mace. editor. New York: Humanities Press, 1957, pp 155-166.

40. The provision to have reasonable grounds for denial rules out the prankster who refuses to heed the ban against shouting "Fire Fire!" in a crowded theater that has no fire. He is making a false claim and one that is likely to be harmful.

and which requires undeniable assent counts against it. If the statement "Atheism is wrong" is affirmed, the test question is: "What reasons would it take to deny your contention that atheism is morally wrong?" Being able to specify suitable rebuttal conditions against one's own position is not a weakness but a way to improve moral deliberation.

The fact that adherents of an affirmation say that it cannot be denied does not imply that it cannot be denied. For the standard of undeniability is the refusal by believers to permit anything to count against their affirmation. While believers affirm their belief, disbelievers deny it with as much ease as is needed to show that it is wrong. If, for example, one claims that (c) "The authority of the Holy Spirit should be taken above the authority of Copernicus" and this is analyzed to mean that (a) "The authority of the Holy Spirit should be above that of Copernicus in deciding whether the world moves;" and according to the Holy Spirit (b) "The world is established that it cannot be moved," then what the Holy Spirit claims is surely false, for it is true that the world moves around the sun. Since (b) is false, and a conjunction is true only if its conjuncts together are true, the *analysandum* (c) of the conjunction (a) and (b) cannot be true.[41]

One could do similar things with the pledge of allegiance. If the statement, "The United States of America is 'one nation under God, indivisible, with liberty and justice for all'" is taken to imply the claim that this is the case and that this ideal is daily achieved or daily being worked for, then it makes a false claim. If one of the conjuncts is false then the conclusion cannot be true. But what makes the pledge immoral is that the claims it makes are not allowed to be denied. More generally, the right to claim that a moral decision is right depends on being willing and able to show grounds for denying it, especially since moral refinement depends on the ability to deny that which in the infinite millennium is fated to be wrong.

Without having ways to deny moral decisions one could not teach one's children to deny what is morally wrong. If, for example, children are taught that questions like "What will happen if I am bad?" "How was I born?" and "How was the world made?" are undeniably answered by "The witches riding their broomsticks will get you," "The stork brought you," and "God made the world in seven days," then they are taught to believe what is wrong: for the witches won't get you because the claim that there are witches is false, for there are no witches; storks no sooner bring babies than shrimps whistle; how the world came about is debatable;

41. This is an application of the truth table for conjunction.

and however long it took, it was not done single-handedly in seven days. This whole batch of beliefs rests on false claims. Though these examples are obvious, if we teach our children that we are "one nation under God" and that the ends of education like "God," "culture," and "virtue" are "undebatable,"[42] as is generally done in schools, just what are we teaching them? To believe that we are "one nation under God" is not a tautology, but a debatable issue and rests on a dubious claim at best.[43]

To teach a child what his elders by word of mouth believe is assuredly the wish of his elders, but is the child thereby taught to seek for and to tell the truth? If we do not in the end teach our children to seek for and to tell the truth, what meaning or credibility will their education have?[44] Yet when we teach our children to grow up believing in the pledge of allegiance, we teach them to overlook what may be false, and when they come to affirm the pledge over and over they no longer come to know quite what it means to be truthful in all things. Unless we teach our children ways of being able to deny what they have been taught to believe, we mock the principle that we ought to teach our children to seek for and to tell the truth. For without teaching them to deny what they come to regard as doubtful or false, they will no longer be able to tell the difference between right and wrong. It is, after all, in the things we do to teach children to look for and to tell the truth that we show that what is good or bad is not our thinking that makes it so. It is in these things we do daily that we show the young what they are to believe.

Since we could never know how to tell the truth without having been taught to do so at an early age, "Teach the children to look for and to tell the truth" is one of the main moral answers to the question "What moral beliefs shall we teach?" For what is esteemed as having the most worth becomes finally the standard for deciding what shall be taught to the young.

Whether a society that encourages truth-telling is better than one that does not, as in Orwell's *1984*, is not at all easy to decide, though we are bound to reap the consequences. It would seem that, except for the most unusual circumstances, opting for non-truth telling, on principle, would cause a great deal of harm.[45]

42. See "The Deeper Problem in Education," Editorial in *Life* reprinted in *The Great Debate: Our Schools in Crisis*, C. W. Scott, C. M. Hill and H. Burns, eds. New York: Prentice Hall, 1959, pp. 35-37. Similar authoritarian practices continue with some citizens' efforts to remove library books, some school board requirements for dress codes, hair lengths, and removal of beards, etc.

43. That we are a nation of "liberty and justice for all" seems hardly appropriate to proclaim daily unless we care to breed a nation of liars and sheep.

44. I share Mill's concern to distinguish truth and falsity. J. S. Mill, *loc. cit.*

45. For an example of an exception to truth-telling my book *(loc. cit.)* pp. 152-153.

But if people decide to live in a society that obligates them to tell the truth, it would be markedly odd for the schools within such a society to profess to teach the truth and yet teach the young to fabricate *a priori* assumptions or tautologies out of moral beliefs. It would be a pity if the children of a generation had not been taught to tell the truth because they were not given a way to deny what was wrong, especially since knowing how to handle the denial sign is a requirement for living in the adult world.

A condition for deciding what moral beliefs to teach is for a believer to provide a Court of Reason analagous to a legal system, acceptable to all parties in a dispute showing what would count as a good reason for a believer to deny his own belief. Otherwise, the moral counterpart to the second rule of adjudication is not fulfilled. Moral and other claims cannot otherwise be judged.

Whatever its limitations, this extension of the falsifiability principle does this much: it punctures the idea of morality being served up as though it were true in about the same way as two plus two equals four or as a definition of a husband as a married man that cannot be denied without self-contradiction. This may be one source of the strength of the older notion that nothing is absolute and that no ends are final. Deniability is simply the anti-finality maxim in moral deliberation. One might come thereby to be restrained in one's thinking from converting moral affirmations or beliefs into tautologies or definitions. For the shift in the use of a claim or belief from sense I to sense II or sense III is capricious.

SYNOPSIS AND CONCLUSION

I have tried to show that there is a difference between right and wrong moral beliefs. I tried to distinguish between belief-in and belief-that by showing that the former often rest on the latter, but that in either case beliefs are used to make claims. One can show how claims are open to appraisal. One cannot always do the same for beliefs. The study of claims shows that there is a difference between making and appraising claims. To appraise them in a legal system presupposes a system of rules for recognition, adjudication and enforcement. With the help of these rules claims in a legal system are appraised and are either affirmed or denied. If consequently moral claims and beliefs are to be taken seriously, there needs to be a system for appraising them.

One way to tell—and hence also to teach—the difference between right and wrong moral beliefs is to find out if they are open to denial. It should be mentioned in this connection that locutions like "I claim" or "I believe," unlike "I know," are open to modification, qualification, rebuttal, or rejection. Judgments made in legal cases are rendered in the form "affirmed" or "upheld" or "denied." Accordingly, the language of claims provides an instructive example in understanding and in teaching moral beliefs, for claims reveal and magnify features of appraisal not readily accessible in the study of beliefs.

Although claims may be used as avowals, they can be true or false, affirmed or denied; they are falsifiable and open to denial. By analogy with claims, moral beliefs are likewise deniable. Appeal to ordinary examples shows that beliefs can be qualified, modified or denied. Avowing beliefs without criteria is like using claims to do nothing more than to bellow in the wild in a childish fashion.

By analogy with claims I tried to show why it is important to be able to deny as well as affirm moral beliefs. Being able to deny moral beliefs rests in part on being able to detect truth claims made or implied by those beliefs. Only if these conditions are fulfilled will we be able, it seems, to distinguish—and also to teach —right from wrong.

Other conditions for teaching the difference between right and wrong are undoubtedly wanting, but in defense of the view that the difference between right and wrong ought to be taught, I have tried to show how, with the aid of the legal language of claims, we can go some of the way toward appraising which moral beliefs should be taught.[46]

If, however, the view continues to prevail that nothing is good or bad but thinking makes it so, and if there is no provision in moral language for saying, "But if the cause be not good" or "But if the pledge be not good," is it any wonder that under some such auspices virtue cannot be taught?

---

46. In the use of claims one can say "no" as well as "yes." One cannot always say "no" to those beliefs that are not allowed to be challenged.

7

Moral Duty and the Academic Scientist

ROBERT D. HESLEP

I

NOT very long ago the duties of academic scientists were commonly agreed upon; and they, as usually conceived, were comparatively minimal. They were, in general, of the sorts ordinarily imputed to all academic researchers, viz. disciplinary and civil. Academic scientists were viewed as obligated to follow the rules of their respective disciplines, and they were regarded as bound to aid their country in times of national crisis. They were not customarily looked upon as having any other type of duty.[1] In recent years, however, this traditional position has been strongly challenged. It has been argued that the position does not recognize that academic scientists now possess a great social influence and, therefore, might very well have new obligations. Moreover, it has been contended that the position is not useful for determining what these new duties, if any, might be. Because of the discontent with the traditional stance, other conceptions of the duties of academic scientists have been offered lately. And, because of the concern with the social influence of academic scientists, a large portion of the alternative conceptions have formulated their obligations as moral ones.

Of the different types of action which have been recently taken as morally binding upon academic scientists, there is one which compels special interest. It is, most generally stated, the academic scientist's publicity of his socially significant discoveries. This form of action has been advanced as a moral obligation of academic scientists by a fair number of academic figures.[2] It calls

1. For a current illustration of the traditional position, see the article concerning Professor Louis Fieser, the inventor of napalm, in *Time* (January 5, 1968), 66ff.

2. Rolf Buchdahl, "An Ethic for the Quiet Revolution"; in *A Guide to Dialogue between Science and Religion,* edited by Rolf Buchdahl and Donald W. Shriver, Jr., on behalf of the Experimental Study of Religion and Society and the Study-Research Group on Science and Theology at North Carolina State University (Raleigh, North Carolina, 1967), pp. 125-131. Herbert C. Kelman, "Manipulation of Human Behavior: An Ethical Dilemma for the Social Scientist," *The Journal of Social Issues,* XXI (April, 1965), 31-46. Leonard Krasner, "The Behavioral Scientist and Social Responsibility: No Place to Hide,"*The Journal of Social Issues,* XXI (April, 1965), 9-30. F. A. Vick, "Science and Its Standards";

to mind several well-known proposals which have been made, by such advocates of democratic society as Thomas Jefferson and John Dewey, on the desirability of the free communication of knowledge within society. And it has been supported by diverse theories of moral duty, including deontological as well as utilitarian ones.

Even though the proponents of the claim that this kind of action is morally obligatory for academic scientists have frequently supported their individual contentions with theoretical ideas, they have given, by and large, very little attention to the fundamental questions pertaining to the claim. As a result, they have usually ignored some serious problems. By specifying these difficulties, one will be in a position to do more than just show that the proponents of the claim have often not defended their conclusions satisfactorily. One will be able, also, to specify basic problems which future advocates of the claim will have to recognize and overcome. A way to locate a number of the difficulties is to examine the arguments which have been offered to justify the claim. Seemingly most of the arguments may be treated as of two types.

II

One type of argument, which is deontological, may be conveniently called "the argument from contract"; for it holds as a major premise that the keeping of contracts, irrespective of consequences, is a moral duty. The academic scientist, according to this sort of argument, is a member of human society and, therefore, is a moral agent. Between the academic scientist and human society there is, at least implicitly, a contract. The academic scientist is primarily concerned with the discovery of knowledge, and human society is interested in utilizing knowledge for its purposes. To foster the pursuit of knowledge, human society has agreed to confer certain freedoms and privileges upon the academic scientist and, furthermore, has demanded that he inform it of any socially significant knowledge which he discovers. And to further his interests, the academic scientist, in turn, has accepted the freedoms and privileges proffered by human society and has consented to inform it of whatever socially significant knowledge he determines. The keeping of contracts is an act which is morally binding in itself; it is obligatory for a moral agent apart from any of its consequences. It follows, therefore, that the academic sci-

in *Moral Education in a Changing Society,* edited by W. R. Niblett. (London: Faber and Faber, 1963), pp. 66-77. Robert Watson-Watt, "Observations on the Ethical Responsibility of the Scientist"; an address to the American Chamber of Commerce Research Association Assembly in June, 1962.

entist ought, morally, to publicize the socially important knowledge which he discovers.

A succinct instance of the argument from contract is furnished
by Sir Robert Watson-Watt.

The ethical responsibility of the scientist, within the definition to which
I have chosen to limit the title of scientst [sic], is, I believe, crystal-clear.
It is this: In recognition of the privileged and endowed freedom of action
he enjoys, he should, after an appraisal that may well be agonizing, declare all the social consequences he may foresee, however dimly, which
are even remotely likely to follow the disclosure not only of his own contributions to science but also of those of other scientists within his wide
sphere of knowledge and competence. He should outline the social good
that he can foresee as resulting from the technological follow-up of "pure"
research; he must outline the potential social evil. He will seldom be qualified to make quantitative estimates, but to the best of his ability he should
define fields and magnitudes. Nothing less can suffice as partial payment
for his privileged tenancy of the Ivory Tower. No plea that he "doesn't
understand politics or economics" that, "even if behavioral science be
a science (which he doubts) he is even further from understanding it,"
should be sustained. We must all do our poor best, with the intelligence
at our disposal, toward mapping the upward, and marking the downward,
slopes on our still long road of social evolution.[3]

Even though Sir Robert speaks of the social good and social evil
which might follow from the application of scientific knowledge,
he clearly does not intend that the promotion of social good or the
mitigation of social evil is a reason why the academic scientist
should, morally, publicize his socially important discoveries. He
plainly posits that the academic scientist is morally bound to do
this solely because he is in contract with human society to do so:
The academic scientist must publicize his socially significant findings in ". . . recognition of the privileged and endowed freedom
of action he enjoys"; only by publicizing them can he make ". . .
partial payment for his privileged tenancy of the Ivory Tower."
Apparently, the possible social good and the possible social evil to
which Sir Robert refers are intended by him to be nothing more
than marks whereby to identify socially significant knowledge.
Regardless of which instance of the argument from contract one
considers, however, it is susceptible to difficulties.

Some might wish to launch an attack upon the argument from
contract by insisting that the notion of a contract between the

---

3. Watson-Watt, *op. cit.* This passage is also quoted by Krasner, *op. cit.*, 27. According
to this passage, Sir Robert holds that an academic scientist is morally bound to publicize
more than *his* socially important research: He is also morally obligated to publicize such
research, within his sphere of knowledgeability, undertaken by *other* scientists. While
this latter alleged obligation is interesting, it is too complex to be discussed in the present
inquiry.

academic scientist (or anyone else) and human society is non-sensical. They might want to point out that the only contract which an academic scientist can be shown to have is one into which he has entered with some legally recognized party, such as a university. Although an attack along this line has to be recognized as striking at the root of the argument from contract, it should not be viewed as necessarily destroying the argument; for it might be charged with treating the argument unfairly. It might be said to beg the question when it says that the concept of a contract between the academic scientist and human society is meaningless, and it might be said to be irrelevant when it talks about contracts whose existence can be verified. Despite any disputes over its soundness, however, an attack of this type does focus upon a problem of the argument from contract. When a person speaks of a contract between an academic scientist (or anyone else) and human society, he is talking, obviously, about a special kind of contract, one whose nature is not ordinarily known; and whether or not he may employ a concept of such a contract in a justification of a statement about the moral duty of the academic scientist depends upon what that concept is. If, for example, the concept portrays the contract as a myth with an explanatory function—a portrayal suggested by a current apologetic interpretation of natural law[4]—the concept is likely to cause one to doubt that any statement of the academic scientist's moral duty resting upon it is satisfactorily justified. Arguments relying upon myths are rarely ever acknowledged, at least ordinarily, to justify their conclusions adequately. Unfortunately, those who have employed the argument from contract have not even intimated the basic views which they severally assume of the contract to which they respectively refer. They leave one wondering if the claim that the academic scientist is morally bound to publicize his socially important findings rests ultimately upon a myth or some other principle whose probative force is equally suspect.

As already mentioned, the statement that the keeping of contracts is binding, apart from any consequences, upon moral agents is a key premise in the argument from contract. It is this statement which makes it obligatory for the academic scientist as a moral agent to fulfill the contract which he is alleged to have with human society. Since the statement is vital to the argument and since it is not self-evidently true, it stands in need of justification. In justifying the statement, one, of course, must discount any consequence of the keeping of the contracts. But if one must do this how

4. John R. Carnes, "Whether There Is a Natural Law," *Ethics*, LXXVII (January, 1967), 122-129.

is he to show that the keeping of contracts is binding upon moral agents? According to the argument from contract, a moral agent is a member of human society. And what does it mean, at least partially, to be a member of human society if not to be a party to contracts? Are not contracts instruments which help to hold human society together? If the answer is affirmative, then it seems to follow that to be a moral agent, at least in part, is to be a party to contracts. And if it is further granted that contracts by their nature are made to be kept, then it also appears to follow that moral agents, being parties to contracts, are bound to keep their contracts.

While this course of thought is pertinent, it is far from compelling; for it contains points which sorely require clarification. It is suggestive to define a moral agent as a member of human society, but it is hardly sufficient. Is the expression "a member of human society" simply another way of saying "a human being," or does it refer to a human being insofar as he has relations with other human beings? Presumably, the latter alternative it to be preferred; for the line of thought in question assumes that to be a member of human society is to have contractual relations. This alternative, however, prompts one to wonder what the relations are between human beings which make them members of human society. On the assumption that being a member of human society entails being a party to contracts, it seems that at least some of these relations are contractual ones. It is not readily evident, on the other hand, what such relations are. The argument from contract, as previously mentioned, views the nature of contracts in an extraordinary way but does not spell out the way specifically. So in its failure to explain adequately why the keeping of contracts is binding upon moral agents, the argument from contract is confronted with the problem of clarifying what a moral agent is. Unfortunately those who have followed this sort of argument do very little in the way of telling what a moral agent is. At most they speak of him as a member of human society or as a social being.

When the argument from contract concludes that the academic scientist is morally obliged to publicize his socially important work, it raises the specter of conflicting duties. The academic scientist, it is commonly recognized, has duties, moral or not, other than that of informing society of his socially relevant work. He has duties to some college or university and to his colleagues; and he may have duties incurred by a commitment to an industrial concern, a publisher, or a governmental agency. Of these duties one or more may conflict with his obligation to publicize his socially significant findings. If, for example, he agrees to undertake for a governmental agency a project involving national security, he might very well be bound by an oath of secrecy which proscribes his publicizing at least some of his socially relevant discoveries made during the course of the project. It is not immediately apparent, therefore, that one is justified in saying that the academic scientist is morally bound to inform society of his socially important work if, in so doing, he might violate some other duty. This difficulty is not insurmountable. First, in order to avoid conflicts between moral and non-moral obligations, the academic scientist, it may be pointed out, must not assume non-moral obligations which oppose his moral ones. Second, if he does find himself in a situation where he has a non-moral duty conflicting with his moral duty to publicize his socially important discoveries, he must uphold the latter duty; for moral obligations, it is usually conceded, are superior to non-moral ones. And, third, if he sees himself in a situation where he has a moral duty opposing his moral duty to inform society of his socially relevant work and one of these duties is superior to the other, he must uphold the one which is superior.[5] Before an academic scientist can follow any of these proposals, he must know what moral duties he has other than publicizing his socially significant findings; and he must know the relative superiority, if any, of his moral obligations to one another. So, in order to justify, satisfactorily, its conclusion that the academic scientist is morally bound to publish his socially important work, an argument from contract has to take into account the problem of the conflict of duties. And in order to do this it must specify what moral obligations the academic scientist has beyond publicizing his socially significant discoveries; and it must delineate the relative superiority, if any, of these obligations to one another.

A number of those employing arguments from contract have utterly ignored the difficulty of conflicting duties. When, for example, Sir Robert Watson-Watt asserts, without qualification, that the academic scientist ought, morally, to ". . . declare *all* the social consequences he may foresee,"[6] he completely disregards the possibility that this obligaion is in opposition to another duty which the academic scientist has. If an academic scientist declares all of the social consequences of his findings in, say, nuclear physics, he might very well publicize information which endangers his country's security and, thus, betray his duty as a citizen. On

5. There is the possibility, of course, that an academic scientist will find himself in a situation where he has a moral duty conflicting with the one to publicize his socially important research and both duties will be equally weighted. If so, he has *prima facie* evidence that his body of moral duties is at least partly unsatisfactory.

6. *Loc. cit.*

the other hand, others who have utilized arguments from contract are sensitive to the problem of opposing obligations; nevertheless, they do not seem to be fully cognizant of its various facets. They do not appear to be aware that the academic scientist can avoid conflicts between his moral and non-moral duties only if he knows what all of his moral duties are; in any case, they attempt to specify only a few of the academic scientist's moral duties. Furthermore, they do not even raise the question of whether or not there might be a conflict among the moral duties of the academic scientist.[7]

Indeed, an argument from contract appears to impose a likely opposition between the academic scientist's putative obligation to publicize the socially important findings of his research and another moral duty which he has. It seems fairly plain that the time and effort which an academic scientist will expend in publicizing the socially significant findings of his research may be little or great. He may do nothing more than write a few articles in the popular press and appear on an occasional television interview program; or he may write some books as well as numerous articles for the popular press, engage in public lectures, seek a wide television coverage, participate in political campaigns, and present his case before governmental agencies. How much time and effort he should spend is contingent, presumably, upon a pair of factors: the number of socially relevant discoveries which he makes and the magnitude of the importance of each of the discoveries. If he makes few socially significant discoveries and none of them is of much moment, he does not need to devote much time and effort to publicizing them; but, if he makes many socially important discoveries, although none of them is of great significance, he has to expend a fair amount of time and effort in publicizing them; and if he makes numerous socially important discoveries and several or all of them are of great moment, he has to expend even more time and effort in publicizing them. As an academic scientist increases his time and effort involved in publicizing his socially relevant work, he will decrease the time and effort available to him to expend in other activities, including his research. Thus, the more numerous and important his past and present socially significant discoveries are, the greater the likelihood that his future research will be curtailed. So, in order to carry out his moral duty of publicizing his socially important research, the academic scientist might very well have to forego, to some extent, the other moral duty which he has by virtue of his contract with human society, viz., to pursue knowledge. Yet it is not any more immediately evident that he is obligated to give preference to the publicizing of

7. Cf., e.g., Buchdahl, *op. cit.*, pp. 127ff.

socially relevant knowledge over the pursuit of knowledge than it is readily evident that he is bound to give preference to the pursuit of knowledge over the publicizing of important knowledge. A measure is wanting to determine which of these duties is superior to the other.

Those following the argument from contract have furnished no evidence that they are even aware that an academic scientist might find a conflict between his moral obligation to publicize his socially relevant knowledge and his moral duty to pursue the truth. When Sir Robert Watson-Watt asserts that an academic scientist ". . . should . . . declare all the social consequences he may foresee, however dimly, which are even remotely likely to follow the disclosure not only of his own contributions to science but also of those of other scientists within his wide sphere of knowledge and competence,"[8] he strongly suggests that an academic scientist's publicization of his socially important knowledge will require much time and effort; but he appears to be oblivious to the possibility that the academic scientist's publicization of such knowledge will, therefore, run counter to his duty to seek the truth. Moreover, those following the argument from contract furnish no standard which is helpful for determining whether the academic scientist's duty to publicize his socially applicable knowledge is superior, inferior, or equal to his obligation to pursue the truth. Even though Sir Robert holds that the duty to publicize is *the* ethical responsibility of the academic scientist, he does not fully clarify what he means by this statement; and he gives no reason to justify it sufficiently.

Finally, the argument from contract is confronted with the problem of whether or not the academic scientist is able to publicize the socially relevant findings of his research. When the argument lays down the premise that the academic scientist has contracted with human society, in return for certain freedoms and privileges, to publicize his socially significant work, it does so on the assumption that human society demands him to publicize such work in return for his being granted the freedoms and privileges. It seems fair to say, then, that if one cannot substantiate this assumption, one cannot view the academic scientist as having a contract with human society to inform it of his socially important discoveries. If human society does demand the academic scientist to publicize his socially applicable knowledge, it should have a reason to think that he is capable of publicizing it. It is plainly absurd for one to demand a person to do something if one has no reason to believe that he can do

8. *Loc. cit.*

it. But what is commonly known about the academic scientist's ability to publicize his socially important findings? It is recognized that some academic scientists have talent for mass communication, but it is also acknowledged that some do not have such talent. If an academic scientist without talent for popular communication does attempt to publicize the social relevance of his findings, he is not likely to put his message across. It is known, furthermore, that any academic scientist has some understanding of society; but it is not allowed that every academic scientist comprehends it very well. For instance, sociologists, economists, and political scientists are generally thought to understand society far better than physicists and chemists. If an academic scientist who does not grasp society competently does talk about the social significance of his research, he is likely to be mistaken and misleading, at least in part, in what he says. There is doubt, accordingly, that human society has a ground for demanding every academic scientist to publicize the social import of his discoveries. Surely, it cannot reasonably make the demand if he has no talent for mass communication and/or has no sound knowledge of society. If, therefore, an argument from contract is to make good the premise that any academic scientist is in contract to inform society of socially relevant scientific discoveries, it must take into account the point that some academic scientists might not be able to do so.

While virtually all of the followers of the argument from contract have ignored the possibility that some academic scientists do not have talent for mass communication, a few of them have entertained the notion that some academic scientists might not have a competent grasp of society. It must be remarked, however, that their responses to this notion do not always attract one's assent. To recur, again, to Sir Robert Watson-Watt: "No plea that . . . [the scientist] 'doesn't understand politics or economics' . . . should be sustained. We must all do our poor best, . . ."[9] There is no question that an academic scientist must do his "poor best" if he is morally obligated to publicize his socially pertinent knowledge, but there is a question of whether or not he is so obligated. Thus Sir Robert's contention that the academic scientist must do his "poor best" begs the question. It presumes that any academic scientist, even one who has an inadequate comprehension of society, is morally bound to inform society of his socially relevant discoveries. But this is precisely the point which it is supposed to demonstrate.

9. Loc. cit.

III

The other type of argument which has been utilized to justify the claim that the academic scientist is morally bound to publicize his socially important work takes a utilitarian view of moral duty, and for convenience it will be called "the argument from freedom." According to an argument of this sort, freedom is a major, if not the, moral good, i.e., a cardinal, if not the, good of moral agents; and it ought, morally, to be protected and nurtured whenever it can be. Science, the argument continues, can affect freedom positively or negatively: It can maintain and increase freedom, or it can diminish it. Although the academic scientist sometimes exercises direct control over the applications of his discoveries and, thereby, how the discoveries will affect the freedom of the members of society, he frequently does not exercise such control. More often than not, governmental officials and industrialists are the ones who immediately determine the applications of science and, thus, its influence upon the freedom of the members of society. Yet even when the academic scientist does not directly regulate the applications of his work, he has a moral duty related to the effect of his discoveries upon the freedom of the members of society. Whether or not he immediately controls the applications of his research, he can inform the members of society of the ways in which his findings might, through application, influence their freedom; and by so informing them he will enable them to take advantage of whatever positive ways there might be and to avoid or at least mitigate whatever negative ways there might be. Consequently, the academic scientist is obligated, as a moral agent, to publicize the various ways in which his discoveries might influence, through application, the freedom of the members of society.

An obvious instance of the argument from freedom is provided by Professor Herbert C. Kelman in a paper dealing with the social responsibility of social scientists. Professor Kelman commences by laying down a set of theoretical moral principles stated in the terms of a species of freedom, viz., the freedom to choose:

. . . the freedom and opportunity to choose is a fundamental value. To be fully human means to choose. Complete freedom of choice is, of course, a meaningless concept. But the purpose of education and of the arrangement of the social order, as I see it, is to enable men to live in society while at the same time enhancing their freedom to choose and widening their areas of choice. I therefore regard as ethically ambiguous any action that limits freedom of choice, whether it be through punishment or reward or even through so perfect an arrangement of society that people do not care to choose.[10]

After an attempt to defend these principles, Professor Kelman proceeds to point out what he takes to be a fact: The social scientist, whether practitioner, applied researcher, or basic researcher, ineluctably contributes, immediately or indirectly, to the manipulation of human behavior, whether that of individuals, groups, or whole societies. Accordingly, Professor Kelman argues, the social scientist is morally obligated to mitigate "the dehumanizing effects of new developments in the field of behavioral change."[11] A step which the social scientist can take in this direction, Professor Kelman proposes, is his increasing other people's active awareness of the manipulative aspect of his work, including the ways in which it might limit their freedom to choose. In short, it is moral duty of the social scientist to publicize the possible manipulative effects of his work. Irrespective of the instance of the argument from freedom which a person considers, however, he will find it liable to problems.

A fairly obvious difficulty is connected with the premise that freedom is morally good. Freedom, it is widely recognized, is a term with different possible meanings; and whether or not freedom is morally good depends, apparently, upon which meaning is intended. At one extreme freedom might be formulated as referring to something which is not necessarily morally worthy. For example, it has been defined by Hobbes as a person's doing whatever he wants to do. At the other extreme, it may be conceived so as to apply to only what is morally estimable. Thus it has been viewed by Aristotle as a person's being able to act virtuously. And at a point perhaps between these extremes it has been construed as referring to something which is a mixture of that which is morally valuable and that which is not necessarily so. Hence, it has been said by Locke to be a person's doing whatever he wants to do short of violating the moral laws of nature. If freedom is taken as involving only what is morally valuable, it may be properly regarded, presumably, as morally good. And if it is held as including something which is not necessarily morally worthy but, in addition, something which is, it may still be properly regarded, seemingly, as morally good. But if it is taken as containing nothing which is necessarily morally worthy, it cannot be viewed as morally good. An argument from freedom, therefore, in order to contend that freedom is morally good and, thus, that the academic scientist ought

10. Kelman, *op. cit.*, 34-35.
11. *Ibid.*, 41.

to foster freedom, must employ a concept of freedom which applies to something which is necessarily morally valuable.

A few of the writers following the argument from freedom have not even tried to clarify the several notions of freedom which they respectively hold; and those who have made the attempt do not always seem to have been cognizant that their individual conceptions of freedom must contain, at least in part, something which is morally estimable. The force of the latter proposition can be emphasized through a brief examination of the defense which Professor Kelman suggests for his principle that the freedom to choose is a fundamental moral good: (1) The desire to choose represents a universal human need; (2) freedom of choice is an inescapable component of other valued states, such as love, creativity, mastery over the environment, and maximization of one's capacities; and (3) the valuing of free individual choice is a vital protection against tyranny.[12] (1) That the desire to choose represents a universal human need implies, apparently, that the freedom to choose is quite pertinent to man's psychological condition; but the statement does not indicate, in an obvious way, that such freedom is morally valuable. Something cannot be said to be morally worthy just because it might satisfy a universal human need. It is not usually thought, for example, that the freedom to have sexual intercourse is necessarily morally good even though it is ordinarily held that the desire for sexual intercourse represents a universal human need. (2) That freedom of choice is essentially integral to other valued states means, perhaps, that such freedom is widely valued; but the statement does not allow one to conclude that such freedom is morally valuable. Love, creativity, and the other valued states to which freedom of choice is said by Professor Kelman to be essentially integral are not necessarily morally valuable in any readily evident way. It is arguable, for example, that some love and some creativity are morally bad. (3) Even if the statement that the valuing of free individual choice is a vital protection against tyranny is true, it does not make plain that freedom of choice, for that reason, is morally good. There is, maybe, little question that tyranny is morally bad; but there is a doubt that something is morally good simply because it is vital to any protection against tyranny. For Plato, at any rate, democracy, which includes the freedom to choose, is morally bad as well as opposed to tyranny.

Yet, even if an argument from freedom utilizes a concept of freedom comprizing something morally worthy, it is liable to be

12. *Ibid.*, 35.

confronted with other problems. Two such problems are similar
to ones related to the argument from contract, namely whether
or not the academic scientist is able to publicize his socially
significant discoveries and whether or not his publicizing them
will conflict with other moral duties.

According to the argument from freedom, the academic scientist ought, morally, to inform the members of society of the ways
in which applications of his research might affect their freedom
because by so informing society he will be fostering freedom,
which is morally good. Consequently the academic scientist is
morally bound to publicize his findings relevant to the freedom
of the members of society only if he is capable of doing so; for,
if he cannot do so, it does not make sense to say that he will not
be able to help promote freedom by doing so. That some academic
scientists have the talent to transmit their socially significant
work through the mass media of communication seems highly
probable, but that all or even a majority of them have such
talent is not at all apparent. Moreover it is granted that some
of them comprehend society competently enough to understand
adequately the social relevance of their inquiries; however,
it is not allowed that all or even a majority of them comprehend
society that well. The argument from freedom, therefore, must
take into account the possibility that only some academic scientists are likely to be capable of publicizing their socially important discoveries. Unhappily, those who have followed the
argument have generally ignored this possibility; virtually all
of them seem to have assumed that any academic scientist has
the required talent for mass communication and has a profound
grasp of society.

With respect to the argument from freedom, freedom is a
cardinal moral good; and whatever act will contribute to freedom is morally obligatory. Thus the academic scientist is
morally bound to publicize his work important for freedom in
society because, thereby, he will help promote freedom. If,
however, the academic scientist will be promoting freedom by
publicizing his discoveries pertinent to freedom in society, he
will also, it seems, be contributing to freedom simply by pursuing
knowledge. At least it is usually recognized that knowledge is
a necessary condition of freedom. As already explained, the publicizing of knowledge and the pursuit of it might very well oppose,
to an extent, one another when they both are undertaken by the
same person. If, consequently, an academic scientist cannot
engage in the publicizing of his discoveries relevant to freedom
in society without interfering with his quest for knowledge, he
faces a possible conflict in moral duties, a conflict which the

argument from freedom must resolve. Practically none of those who follow the argument entertains, let alone resolves, the conflict.

Finally, an argument from freedom, even when it employs a concept of freedom embodying something morally valuable, is likely to encounter a difficulty connected with how the word "good" is used. A key premise in such an argument is the statement, "Freedom is morally good"; but, as it stands, the premise is obscure. In the past, the word "good" has been assigned different functions by different ethicists; and, as it appears in the premise, it might have any one of these functions or some other. If, furthermore, it functions in the premise in any of several definite ways, it will pose a knotty problem for the argument to which the premise belongs. This point can be clarified, to an extent, by a brief examination of three various interpretations of the word.

Some philosophers, e.g., G. E. Moore, have held that the word "good" refers to a simple property which supervenes upon certain objects. And, in keeping with this position, they have contended that in any true statement of the form, "X is good," the word "good" refers not to any property integral to the subject but to a property which supervenes upon it. Accordingly, in the premise, "Freedom is morally good," the word "good" is to be interpreted as referring to a property which supervenes upon freeedom whenever it is possessed by moral agents. Since the property good is simple, it cannot be analyzed into parts and, thus, cannot be analytically defined. As a result, Moore and others argue, one cannot state, in any helpful way, what good is; ultimately, one can say only that good is good. Nevertheless, it is insisted by these philosophers, good can be known, albeit by intuition alone. It follows, then, that the truth of any statement of the form, "X is good," must be known by intuition. If, therefore, the proposition, "Freedom is morally good," is true, it must be known as true by intuition: One must intuit that good does supervene upon freedom whenever it is had by moral agents. Even though intuition has been used as a cognitive principle by a notable number of philosophers, it is a term whose meaning is not readily evident. At least it is not at all obvious what it means to intuit that freedom is good, morally or otherwise.

Other ethicists, such as A. J. Ayer and Charles Stevenson, have held that the word "good," rather than being significant of anything, is purely emotive. It may vent a feeling of satisfaction; it might express a positive attitude toward a given subject; or it may serve to elicit from a given audience a favorable attitudinal response toward a given subject. But it will never convey any meaning. In the premise, "Freedom is morally good," accordingly, the word "good" has nothing more than an emotive force. More specifically, it functions to persuade the members of a given audience to desire the possession of freedom by moral agents. Since the emotive interpretation of the word "good" leads to the position that the premise, "Freedom is morally good," is primarily an instrument of persuasion, it prompts one to question how soundly the premise helps to support the claim that the academic scientist is morally obligated to publicize his work pertinent to freedom in society. Also it causes one to wonder if the argument from freedom is mainly a persuasive device.

A third group of philosophers, including most notably R. M. Hare, argue that the word "good" in its central usage is employed in view of guiding, directly or indirectly, behavior, to commend an object with regard to its excellences, or "good-making" characteristics. And, consequently, they contend that in any statement of the form, "X is good," the word "good" is being used to praise the subject in view of its excellences. So in the premise, "Freedom is morally good," the word is utilized to commend freedom for certain of its properties to moral agents so as to guide their behavior. When a person commends an object to another in view of directing the latter's behavior, he appears to be saying that the latter person should pursue, preserve, or in some other way act positively toward the object. When, therefore, one states that freedom is morally good and, thereby, praises it with respect to guiding the actions of moral agents, one seems to be saying that moral agents ought to foster, maintain, pursue, and in other ways act positively toward freedom. If so, there seems to be a circularity in the argument from freedom. Holding a utilitarian notion of moral duty, the argument defines moral duty in terms of the morally good: What one ought to do, morally, is to pursue, preserve, etc., the morally good. But by adopting the commendatory interpretation of the word "good," the argument appears to define the morally good in terms of moral duty. The moral good is whatever a moral agent ought to attain, foster, etc. Insofar as an argument formulates moral duty in terms of the morally good and states the latter in terms of the former, it is plainly employing circular definitions.

There is no indication that the writers making use of arguments from freedom have seriously considered how they utilize the word "good" in their respective premises. In any of the arguments, there is no mention of how the word functions; and it is possible to regard the word, as it appears in the argument, as having different but incompatible functions. Since these authors have not scrutinized how they use the word "good" in their several arguments, they have not tried to overcome any of the sorts of difficulties attendant to the various possible functions of the word.

IV

In resumé, diverse fundamental problems have been shown to confront two types of arguments which have been put forth to contend that academic scientists are morally bound to publicize their socially pertinent discoveries. Any argument from contract must make plain what it means by the principle contract and by the term moral agent. Any argument from freedom must employ a concept of freedom which is not only clear but also morally substantive, and it must take into account the difficulties which might arise in its use of the word "good." And arguments of both kinds have to overcome problems of conflict in moral duties and the ability of the academic scientist to inform society of socially important scientific work.

A couple of these difficulties appear to be especially connected with the arguments of the two sorts just mentioned. At least, an explication of the principle contract seems to be a problem mainly for arguments from contract; and a proper formulation of the principle freedom appears to be a difficulty primarily for arguments from freedom. But the other problems need not be regarded as confined chiefly to one or the other of these types of arguments. While an explanation of the term moral agent is a difficulty for the argument from contract, it seems to be one for the argument from freedom as well as for any other sort of argument concerned with whether or not the publicization of socially relevant scientific findings is a moral duty of academic scientists. To talk about any moral duty of an academic scientist or anyone else is to talk about a duty of a moral agent and, thus, to pose the question of what a moral agent is. While the difficulties involved in the use of the word "good" are related to arguments from freedom, they pertain to any argument which is concerned with any moral duty of the academic scientist and which relies upon a utilitarian notion of duty. Any such argument conceives moral duty with respect to what is morally good and, therefore, is susceptible to problems in the use of the word "good." While the possibility of conflict in moral duties and the doubtful ability of the academic scientist to publicize his socially important work are difficulties of the argument from contract and the argument from freedom, they appear to relate to any kind of argument propounding that the academic scientist is morally obliged to publicize his socially significant work.

Normally, a moral agent, however conceived, is regarded as having a multiplicity of duties; hence, to urge one type of action as a moral duty of the academic scientist is to propose a duty which might oppose some other which he has as a moral agent. And whether or not the academic scientist is capable of publicizing his socially important research is a question of fact; consequently, it may arise irrespective of the principles of one's argument.

8

Normative Discourse and Education

GEORGE L. NEWSOME, JR.

EDUCATION is a normative, even moral, as well as intellectual enterprise. For better or worse, education helps to shape character and conduct. This fact is evident in many discussions of education be they at the practical or theoretical level. For this reason, it seems that the language in which education is discussed is incurably normative.[1] In the educational enterprise moral and normative considerations are not easily avoided.

The use of normative language in the practical affairs of schooling is readily observable. Teachers frequently use normative language to direct and control conduct. Words like "right," "wrong," "ought," "responsibility," "duty," "justice," "injustice," "good," and "bad" frequently are used in contexts that indicate that the purpose is to modify conduct, direct it along lines thought to be conducive to the purposes of schooling, or to instill certain values and beliefs. Moral language is also used to appraise conduct and to sanction or disapprove it. Finally, normative language is used to give reasons both for and against prescriptions and evaluations.

The importance of moral and ethical considerations in education is evident in the vast amount of literature on the subject. Much of the literature concerns practical problems of social control and discipline. There is also a considerable body of literature dealing with descriptive ethics. This is often found in sociological and psychological studies of schools and schooling, studies of teachers' personalities, attitudes, and beliefs, and of the role of the school in the community. There is also considerable literature dealing with moral and spiritual values in education, with character training, and with philosophical views of morals and ethics in education.

It is not the purpose of this paper, however, to review the literature on morals and ethics in education or offer analysis

---

1. L. M. Brown, *General Philosophy in Education*. (New York: McGraw-Hill, 1966, pp. 182-183.

and criticism of it. Instead, an attempt will be made to briefly sketch out some of the moral and ethical challenges to education at the present time, demonstrate difficulties in moral and ethical discourse about education, and explicate a framework for philosophical study of morals and ethics in education.

MORAL AND ETHICAL CHALLENGES TO EDUCATION

Some of the more challenging issues facing society and education today are moral in character. The civil rights movement, the desegregation and integration of schools, a host of court decisions in favor of individual rights, programs for the disadvantaged and the poor, protests and demonstrations, and even riot and rebellion all point to a growing dissatisfaction with what are felt to be injustices. The younger generation is aware of moral issues. Some oppose war on moral grounds and many more find moral short-comings in government, business, and educational institutions. The established order of things is increasingly being subjected to evaluation and criticism. Schools, as the very training ground of the establishment and the ultimate hope for its perpetuation, may yet face much more serious challenges to their authority.

It is against the moral challenges of the time and against the prospect for even more deliberate and intense moral challenges to education that the issues of moral and ethical discourse in education may be viewed. That the challenge is to the established order indicates that the place to begin is not with esoteric moral and ethical theories or with the technical aspects of moral and ethicals language, but rather with the "mud sills" of morality in education. The foundation of morality in education, as in the dominant groups of the society who control education, is the conventional morality of the middle class.[2] This fact must be faced whether one wishes to recommend an ethical theory or engage in metaethical analysis.

The conventional morality is not so much the morality exhibited in behavior as it is the morality and values professed. It is the mores, or more particularly, the attitudes and beliefs rooted in custom and tradition. It is a nebulous morality. It is a hodge-podge, a residue distilled from many sources such as Christianity, capitalism, and a variety of homespun traditions. Not only is it nebulous, but it is also varied, filled with platitudes, beset with inconsistencies, and frequently just plainly hypocritical. Justifications of it are often romantic and doctrinaire. Some of

2. Robert J. Havighurst and Bernice L. Neugarten, *Society and Education*. Boston: Allyn and Bacon, 1967, p. 449.

these portray democracy as a set of doctrines lending support to an idealized version of status quo middle class virtues. Whatever the justification, the morality does not conform to many of the facts of life as those facts are faced by men.

Schools, as social institutions, conserve, simplify, and purify the conventional morality which they attempt to transmit to or even inculcate into the young. At the same time, in the interest of mass production they resort to a considerable amount of regimentation and evolve an educational bureaucracy. The simplified and purified view of conventional morality and the requirements of regimentation and bureaucracy are not always compatible. When this occurs, schools seem to violate in practice the principles that they teach or indoctrinate. The school is then forced to appeal to a morality of institutions (or a corporate morality) as opposed to an individual morality. This double standard of morality, one for individuals and another for institutions, is common in American life.

Most of the features of American middle class morality, including simplified and purified forms taught in schools and the institutional or corporate form, are too well-known to deserve special attention here. Virtues such as hard work, responsibility for one's acts, loyalty, proper recognition and respect for authority, respect for property, honesty, cleanliness, reverence, moderation, and the like are traditionally acclaimed, if not always practiced. Educational institutions are expected to teach these virtues directly by formal instruction, teach them indirectly by example, make them guiding principles in the conduct of education, use them as sanctions, and, when the need arises, enforce them as law. Needless to say, educational institutions are in a sense guardians of middle class morality, and are thereby expected to be considerably more moral than the middle class as a whole.

Because the morality of the school is purer than that of the community, youth from elementary school through college find that the yoke of school discipline sometimes binds and chafes. This is true of students from all social classes, but more so with those from the lower classes.[3] As students progress through school they become better able to spot shortcomings in the morality underlying discipline. These shortcomings may produce puzzlement. For example, young children are reported to experience difficulty in understanding the difference between dishonesty

3. Harold W. Bernard, *Psychology of Learning and Teaching.* New York: McGraw-Hill, 1965, p. 373, shows that a large per cent of lower class youth drop out of school and among the factors influencing dropping out are their "orientation toward the value of education," appropriateness of the curriculum, and treatment by the teacher.

and tact.[4] Adolescents are often said to be concerned with developing their own moral values and are particularly sensitive to moral issues. College students often find the college environment a challenge to their values. They may adopt for a time and then cast off value beliefs in their readjustment to a broader culture and wider range of values.

Youth are also concerned with large social issues and sometimes become passionate devotees of schemes for curing social ills. Today, as always, there are social ills and schemes proposed for curing them. Because of mass media, social issues are dramatized as never before. With the drastic increase in college enrollment, American colleges and universities are also developing an intellectual fringe of "drop-in" and pseudo-professional students. European and Latin American universities have always had such students who mingle education with politics and who organize and lead student rebellions against the government and against the university administration.

Moral and ethical challenges to education grow out of larger social issues and out of education itself. Contrary to some popular ideas about education as a panacea for social and moral problems, education itself creates social and moral issues. Schools in America, similar to those envisioned in Plato's *Republic,* help to create and perpetuate social classes.[5] By so doing, schools contribute to inequality among people. Schools train up an educated elite, teach ideas that both promote and retard social progress, and indirectly through teaching and research create conditions which pose new social and moral problems. As one of the leading advocates of education as an instrument of social progress has said:[6]

. . . if we once start thinking no one can guarantee where we shall come out, except that many objects, ends and institutions are surely doomed. Every thinker puts some portion of an apparently stable world in peril and no one can wholly predict what will emerge in its place.

DIFFICULTIES IN MORAL AND ETHICAL DISCOURSE IN OR ABOUT EDUCATION

Granting that education is a moral and ethical enterprise and that it creates many of its own such problems, one may be inclined to examine in greater detail the moral and ethical problems, ana-

4. Karl C. Garrison, Albert J. Kingston, and Arthur S. McDonald, *Educational Psychology.* New York: Appleton-Century-Crofts, 1964, p. 298.

5. Havighurst and Neugarten, *op. cit.,* ch. 3, pp. 69-94, "The School as a Sorting and Selecting Agency."

6. John Dewey, *Experience and Nature.* Chicago: The Open Court Publishing Company, 1925, p. 222.

lyze the moral and ethical language used, or make moral and ethical judgments about education. In doing any one or all of these things, it may be helpful to first determine the criteria for moral and ethical discourse and specify some of the more common contexts in which education is practiced or discussed.

Words such as "moral" or "ethical," "good," or "bad," and "right" or "wrong" tend to be vague and ambiguous. Their meanings are often unclear in specific contexts. For example, "moral" may refer to acts, to sentences, or even to thoughts. Because of the relation of morals to mores, morals and ethics can be studied from the perspectives of social sciences such as anthropology, sociology, psychology. In contrast to these more empirical studies, morals and ethics can be studied philosophically. Moral philosophy, for example, has often been viewed as practical wisdom about how one *ought* to live rather than how men *do in fact* live. The so called practical wisdom of moral philosophy is often supported and reinforced, however, by moral argument or justification and by ethical theories. In the context of theories, moral and ethical terms tend to have theoretical meanings that are different from their more common or ordinary ones.

Because moral and ethical terms may have technical meanings in the contexts of theories, it is sometimes suggested that there is a technical language of morals and ethics. That is, one can speak of the language of morals and ethics as one would of the language of mathematics or the language of chemistry. This analogy, however, is rather weak, for it is doubtful that there are many uniquely moral or ethical terms or that they have highly refined and standardized meanings. As a result, it is difficult to specify any truly adequate set for criteria for moral and ethical discourse.

Distinctions have been made in moral and ethical discourse and criteria have been offered on the basis of them. Many of the distinctions and criteria are useful even though they may not be truly adequate. For example, one writer distinguishes morals from ethics in the following way:[7]

Morals—people's beliefs about right and wrong, good and bad, punishment and desert, and so on, together with their actions in consequent of the beliefs—are human phenomena which are there to be studied and would be there even if nobody were interested in studying them. Ethics uses them as materials for study, just as biology uses living organisms as its materials for study.

When the question arises of how to distinguish between the moral

7. John Hospers, *Human Conduct*. New York: Harcourt, Brace, and World, 1961, p. 5.

and nonmoral, the same writer admits great difficulty because ". . . different people have different views on this point."[8]

Another writer is of the opinion that what he calls "normative ethics" can be subsumed under three general questions: (1) What is right and wrong? (2) What is blame worthy and praiseworthy? (3) What is desirable or worth-while?[9] He also offers four criteria for moral discourse, the first three of which he calls necessary: (1) objectivity or publicly warrantable, (2) universality, (3) practicality, (4) antonomous mode of discourse in that no moral statement is derived from or dependent upon a nonmoral one.[10]

A third author takes a more pessimistic view. He is of the opinion that moral philosophy in this century has been "remarkably barren" and that:[11]

. . we must start from the recognition that there is something peculiarly puzzling and problematic, peculiarly *arguable* about the whole phenomenon of morals. . . . So much is unclear; so many different views have been taken—and not only, of course, about what is morally right or wrong, but about *what it is to be* morally right or wrong.

The same author further states that "When we talk about 'morals' we do *not* all know what we mean; what moral problems, moral principles, and moral judgments are is *not* a matter so clear that it can be passed over as a simple datum."[12]

Although there are, no doubt, some points of agreement among the three authorities cited, there are also noticeable differences. The differences are probably sufficient to indicate that morals and ethics are controversal matters. The differences are also marked enough to raise reasonable doubt about the adequacy of criteria for moral discourse.[13]

Virtually the same things could be said about education. The term "education" encompasses every form of schooling, all levels of schooling, and every aspect of schooling. It is also used to refer to any kind of learning. It is used to refer to both the process of learning or schooling and to the product. It denotes a profession, a body of knowledge, and a wide range of institutions. As a subject of conversation, education can be discussed in a folksy nontechnical way or in terms of abstract theories and doctrines. Some writers distinguish education from learning that results

8. *Ibid.*, p. 8.

9. *Encyclopedia of Philosophy.* New York: Macmillan Company and the Free Press, 1967, Vol. 3, p. 121.

10. *Ibid.*, p. 127.

11. G. J. Warnock, *Contemporary Moral Philosophy*. New York: St. Martin's Press, 1967, pp. 1, 73.

12. *Ibid.*, p. 75.

13. There seems to be kind of inclusiveness, even problematic aspect of moral language that allows one person to interpret a sentence as having moral force and another to interpret it as nonmoral. This may indicate a psychological aspect of language.

from unplanned experiences; others distinguish it from training, and still others, stressing manner of instruction, distinguish it from indoctrination.

That education may be discussed in terms of theories or doctrines seems to suggest a technical language of education. This view is reinforced by works purporting to examine the language of education,[14] by the presence of a *Dictionary of Education*,[15] and by the belief that words such as "teacher," "teaching," "learning," and "curriculum" have technical meanings. On the other hand, most of the theories, much of the technical language, and some of the doctrines are not particularly educational in character but have been taken from more basic disciplines, especially from the social sciences. Indeed, education has been heavily psychologized, almost to the point of becoming applied psychology.

One of the major problems in educational discourse is that the language used is a hodge-podge of technical and non-technical terms employed in ways that are often different from their more ordinary uses or uses in other disciplines. Moreover, there are few, if any, standard uses for them in educational discourse. For example, the word "learning" is used in many ways. Many educators, because of their study of learning theories, attempt to speak of learning as that word is used by learning theorists. Yet to say that "Johnny learned to read" is not at all like saying some of the things learning theorists say when their half-starved or abused rats satisfy specified conditions in a highly controlled laboratory environment. On the other hand, the word "learning" is often used so broadly as to be virtually a synonym for "education."

Much more could be said about both moral and ethical discourse and about educational discourse. Perhaps enough has been said, however, to indicate the complexity of moral and ethical discourse in or about education. This type of discourse is so complex that numerous distinctions must be made in order to sort out some of the more common features and sketch out a scheme for dealing with them. The remaining portion of this paper will briefly survey this task.

A Framework for Philosophical Study of Moral and Ethical Discourse in Education

Assuming that the bed rock of morals and ethics is mores or people's beliefs about right and wrong, good and bad, and their

14. Israel Scheffler, *The Language of Education*. Springfield, Illinois: Charles C. Thomas Publisher, 1960.

15. Carter Good, ed, *Dictionary of Education*. New York: McGraw-Hill, 1959.

actions in consequent of these beliefs, then empirical knowledge of morals and ethics is the concern of the social sciences. In the case of education, empirical knowledge of schooling and the conditions under which it is practiced, including beliefs of its functionaries, patrons, and the like would be matters for scientific study. A considerable body of knowledge on these matters is available, and shows a prevailing middle class morality as previously discussed.

Given a fairly reliable body of knowledge about morals and ethics in the practical affairs of schooling, one need not quibble about whether there is moral knowledge, or about whether morals are matters of practical wisdom. On strictly philosophical grounds, one need not be concerned with how moral and ethical discourse is used by teachers or students in the practical affairs of schooling. This is a matter best studied empirically rather than philosophically. There is, of course, no prohibition upon philosophers doing empirical research, if they are properly trained to do so, but in doing empirical research they are not doing what is usually called philosophy.

Teaching is also a practical matter that can best be studied empirically. The art of teaching has sometimes been called "pedagogy." Pedagogy is largely a matter of skill. Pedagogical skills are learned through imitation and practice. Among pedagogical skills are those relating to effective use of moral and ethical language in the control and direction of conduct. Since the emphasis is upon effective use, the language employed can best be judged in terms of its consequence. The principal consequences are its effects upon students. Therefore, the effectiveness of moral and ethical discourse in teaching is largely a matter for psychological rather than philosophical study.

In addition to the practical art of pedagogy, there is more abstract knowledge *about* it. This knowledge could be called pedagogical knowledge. A considerable portion of educational literature is about the practical arts of schooling such as teaching, curriculum planning, and administration. An examination of this literature reveals that it contains descriptive accounts of practices, rules for various procedures, lists of criteria for good practices, evaluations of practice, discussions of theories and doctrines, and a variety of recommendations.

Where practice itself is based to a considerable degree upon prudence and custom, pedagogical knowledge provides a broader context in which practice can be critically examined and evaluated. For example, practices may be viewed against social demands for education, against scientific knowledge, against professional ethics, or against a wide variety of theories, doctrines, or expectations. Evaluations of these kinds are usually employed for the purpose of giving a broad view of practice and for estimating how well practice measures up to certain external criteria.

One of the major problems in pedagogical knowledge is that of meaningfully relating pedagogical practice to a wide array of external criteria. For example, how can learning theory, or human growth and development, or statistics, or a conception of democracy be meaningfully related to pedagogy? What do these subjects, as known to authorities in the field, have to do with pedagogy? It is doubtful that theories in these subjects, or statements taken from them, logically imply any pedagogical practice. These subjects can, however, be used as criteria against which pedagogy can be judged, but the relevance of the criteria can often be seriously questioned. When the criteria may be relevant, it is difficult to prescribe new pedagogical practices on the basis of judging old ones against the criteria. For example, it is widely held that children differ in rates and patterns of growth and development. Psychology also shows many other differences. On this basis should educators be told "You ought to provide for individual differences in all practical aspects of schooling?"

It is often thought inadvisable to urge people to do what they cannot do. Can schools, as they are known today, really provide for all individual differences, meet all the need of youth, raise standards and curtail drop outs, and insure a balanced curriculum? Perhaps none of these things can really be done.[16] To prescribe that they ought to be done may not be useful advice. There are many empty prescriptions in pedagogical knowledge,[17] some of which function as slogans,[18] and some of which are dignified as aims of education, on the grounds that aims ought to be lofty and inspirational.

Most of what is called pedagogical knowledge is a kind of strained, low level, technology. It is strained in that the application from more basic disciplines to pedagogy is not clear, often of questionable relevance, and of dubious worth to practical educators. It is low level in that pedagogy is a practical art that can be enhanced only in a limited way by knowledge from other disciplines.

There is also a body of knowledge about education that is not directly dependent upon schooling or pedagogy. This is the kind

16. B. Paul Komisar, "Needs and the Needs Curriculum" in *Language and Concepts in Education*, edited by B. Othanel Smith and Robert H. Ennis, Chicago: Rand McNally and Company, 1961, pp. 24-42.

17. Edward Best, "The Empty Prescription in Educational Theory," *Universities Quarterly*, Vol. 14 (June, 1960), pp' 233-242.

18. B. Paul Komisar and James E. McClellan, "The Logic of Slogans" in Smith and Ennis, *loc. cit.*, pp. 195-214.

of knowledge that arises from the study of education as a subject. Portions of educational psychology, the history of educational ideas, basic educational research, and philosophy of education may be cases in point. It may well be that many scholarly disciplines grew out of practical arts and evolved into subjects studied in their own right. In this respect education is perhaps no exception.

Granting much more could be said about education in its various forms, perhaps enough has been said to explicate a scheme for philosophical analysis of normative langage in education.

Analysis of moral and ethical language in education will emphasize *use;* not the use of moral and ethical language by teachers or school officials, but the use of moral and ethical expressions in the literature of education. For example, uses such as prescribing, advising, recommending, appraising will be featured. Since moral and ethical language is also used in arguments and/or in justifications, logical uses will be studied. The logic of the use of expressions (that is, rules for proper use), the informal logic of fallacies, and even the formal logic of argument will come into play.

Philosophical analysis can do little toward clarification of pedagogy, or the practical art of teaching. The effectiveness of the teacher's use of moral and ethical language is largely psychological. On philosophical grounds, one could perhaps point out that self-contradictory moral and ethical utterances or rules cannot be obeyed, that inconsistent sets of moral and ethical rules lead to confusion, and that moral and ethical pronouncents can be meaningfully directed only to moral agents. In the interest of meaning and consistency, it could be pointed out that advising one to do what he cannot refrain from doing, or not to do what he cannot possibly do, is useless.[19] Also in the interest of consistency and to give force to moral rules, the rules may best be put in universal form. For example, if stealing is held to be bad, then it is bad no matter who does it, or whether only a little stealing or a lot of stealing is done. In the application of the rule, if reprimand or punishment is to be inflicted, consistency of application suggests that the reprimand or punishment fit the circumstances of the offense.

Although there may be good reasons for a very limited analysis of moral and ethical language used in pedagogy, it is in the larger context of pedagogical knowledge that moral language, justifications, arguments, value criteria, and value judgments are

19. Paul Taylor, *Normative Discourse.* Englewood Cliffs, N.J.: Prentice-Hall, 1961, p. 208.

related. It is here that the expressed school morality and pedagogy meet. It is here that standards or criteria, both those internal to the educational process and those external to it, come into sharper focus. It is here that the residue of philosophies, shop-worn ethical theories, descriptive accounts of practice, and a host of theories, ideas, terms, and the like borrowed from other disciplines are found.

There is also a history of pedagogical knowledge. An examination of this history reveals many movements and events, the ideas of numerous reformers, a wide variety of doctrines, and the like. An acquaintance with the history of pedagogical knowledge better enables one to recognize the residue of movements, ideas, and doctrines. For example, the romantic naturalism of Rousseau, the sense realism of Pestalozzi, the apperceptive psychology of Herbert, the mysticism of Froebel, and the instrumentalism of Dewey have left a residue of ideas and terminology in pedagogical knowledge. Schemes and movements such as the free school movement, the guidance movement, the Ethical Culture movement, Progressive Education, the Quincy plan, the Winetka plan, the Dalton plan, and many more have also left a residue of terminology and ideas.

Some examples from the language frequently employed in works on pedagogical knowledge may help to illustrate both the residue of ideas and terminology and also issues in moral language. A text on methods of teaching has the following to say about obstacles to mental functioning:[20]

Thus, the teacher without any loss of scholarly dedication, is presented with an added obligation to assure that the interacting student is biologically and psychologically ready to react maturely to the learning content of the curriculum.

In this passage the word "obligation" seems to suggest a moral obligation or duty, but expressions such as "interacting student," "biologically and psychologically ready," "react maturely," and "learning content of the curriculum" obscures the whole passage. The concept of interacting is one common to both Dewey's philosophy and psychology, the concept of readiness has had a long history from Rousseau to modern child psychology, "maturity" is a concept taken from developmental psychology, and "learning content" is an odd expression of curriculum planners. Given this jumble of terminology, most of which is extremely vague and ambiguous, how would a teacher determine his moral obligation? The author of the passage further states:[21]

20. Gail M. Inlow, *Maturity in High School Teaching*. Englewood Cliffs, N.J.: Prentice-Hall, 1964, p. 438.
21. *Ibid.*, p. 439.

The obvious implication of this commission reverts once more to the wholeman concept, which premises that students are totalities, not additive sums of many parts.

The specific message to the teacher here is that he cannot ignore the interlocking relationship among the physical, emotional, social, and mental components.

The "implication" here is hardly more than a vague suggestion. It is far from obvious. The old notion of wholeman is brought up and related to some sort of gestaltan. Finally, what first appeared to be a moral obligation ends up as an apparent fact that one cannot ignore. If it cannot be ignored, then why the "message?" If the teacher has an obligation to do something about the situation, then how can he determine what to do in view of all the interacting and biological and psychological components? Is this a case of an empty prescription?

In the same text, what appears to be a moral question is stated as follows: "Since sex is a wholesome function, why shouldn't it be faced in a mature way at the knowledge-learning level?"[22] The expression "mature way" is ambiguous. Nothing much could be gained from analyzing "knowledge-learning level" in terms of Gilbert Ryle's distinction between "knowing that" and "knowing how." The reader is further informed that, "Within the framework of minimum restrictions, . . . adolescents should be encouraged to associate with members of the opposite sex. . . ."[23] Minimum restrictions are not specified, but an appeal is made to "the standard of the 'reasonable man',", who is identified as "mythical character," one who would "relegate Mrs. Grundy to oblivion," but who would not "be receptive to an ultra-liberal replacement."[24]

There are many other statements in pedagogical knowledge which are in a hypothetical form and appear to be prudential in character. But, in view of the prevailing middle class morality of the school and its allegiance to middle class values, some of these statements may be moral in character. This is particularly the case with literature directed almost exclusively to practical educators. For example, it has been said that "In view of current data concerning the influx of youth into adulthood and the shrinking market for unskilled workers it becomes urgent for teachers at all levels to seek to encourage values that will keep young people in school."[25] Why this should be done is not clear from the context. Is it for individual welfare? Is it for national welfare?

22. *Ibid.*, p. 205.
23. *Ibid.*
24. *Ibid.*
25. Bernard, *op. cit.*, p. 375.

Is it that unemployment is associated with idleness and irresponsibility— disvalues in the middle class system of values? Assuming that practical educators, as agents of the establishment (public servants), feel it to be their duty to serve the national interest, individual welfare, or middle class values, the statement may have moral force.

There are numerous cases in the literature of pedagogical knowledge where words or phrases that are generally prescriptive or commendatory appear to be used largely to win general approval or for rhetorical effect. Perhaps these are emotive uses of moral language and are not limited to any particular field of study.

In addition to pedagogical knowledge, education can be studied as a subject in its own right with little or no regard to schooling as it is practiced. On this level, what is called philosophy of education has typically included moral and ethical aspects of education. Some works in the field have been normative and moralistic. Though it has been said that philosophers are not especially qualified to pontificate on moral issues,[26] some appear to do so with a feeling of immunity from error. Since they may not feel bound by the realm of contingent experience, the following passages from Kant may be a rationale for their views.

. . . Once we are outside the circle of experience, we can be sure of not being *contradicted* by experience. The charm of extending our knowledge is so great that nothing short of encountering a direct contradiction can suffice to arrest us in our course; and this can be avoided, if we are careful in our fabrications—which none the less still remain fabrications.[27]

Perhaps the trouble with some moral philosophies of education is that the "fabrications" are not clearly identified as such and are not allowed to remain fabrications. There seems to be a tendency to see the highly abstract and utopian principles reflecting an underlying reality of practice, or perhaps, imperfectly embodied in it.[28]

There is, of course, metaethical analyses of moral and ethical discourse in education. These analyses presuppose a normative

26. H. S. Eveline, "Some Patterns of Justification in Ethics," *Proceedings of the Aristotelian Society,* (New Series, Vol. 66, 1966), pp. 151.

27. Immanuel Kant, "Introduction to the 'Critique of Pure Reason'" in *A Modern Introduction to Philosophy* edited by Paul Edwards and Arthur Pap. New York: The Free Press, 1965, pp. 615-616.

28. There are numerous works that seem to exhibit this tendency. Among them are Ephraim Vern Sayers and Ward Madden, *Education and the Democratic Faith* (New York: Appleton-Century-Crofts, 1959) and John L. Childs, *Education and Morals* (New York: Appleton-Century-Crofts, 1950).

ethic which has been identified as a purified version of middle class values and morals. Descriptive accounts of it are readily available in sociological and psychological studies of educators and of schooling. Since there is nothing much to be gained by analyzing descriptive accounts of morality and value beliefs, metaethical analysis usually begins with the literature of pedagogical knowledge. It does not limit itself to this level, however, for analysis of moral philosophy of education, and even analyses of analyses are often held to be profitable. Where there is confusion resulting from language or logic, where clarity and precision may be gained from analysis, or where explication and elucidation may reveal the meaning of moral concepts or the characteristics of moral reasoning, metaethical analysis may be appropriately employed. To these ends, the language of education, both as represented in pedagogical knowledge and philosophy of education, especially moral and ethical language, moral and ethical justifications, and/or moral and ethical arguments seem to offer challenging sugject matter for metaethical analysis.

To very briefly summarize the scheme for a philosophical study of moral and ethical language in education, the following points can be made:

1. That education is a moral as well as intellectual enterprise.

2. Conventional morality tends to be accepted, more or less uncritically unless challenged.

3. The conventional morality, the prevailing morality, in America is middle class.

4. A purified and simplified version of this morality and value system is the prevailing and predominant morality and value system of schools at all levels.

5. That middle class values and morals are being seriously challenged, and with them, the simplified and purified version characteristic of educational institutions.

6. That middle class values and morals, including the simplified and purified version taught in schools and colleges, is vague, ambiguous, inconsistent, and often plainly hypocritical.

7. That regimentation, bureaucracy, and the conduct of schooling often compromises the very values and morals proclaimed.

8. That though schooling or education contributes to the solution of sóme moral problems, it creates more of its own.

9. That the moral language of the teacher can best be studied empirically.

10. That pedagogy, the practical art of teaching, is largely a matter of skill, not a matter of philosophy.

11. That pedagogical knowledge, or knowledge about pedagogy and practical affairs of education, is a hodge-podge of knowledge drawn from many disciplines.

12. That a metaethical analysis of pedagogical knowledge may be useful in explicating the meaning of moral concepts and in elucidating moral reasoning in education.